What Others Are Saying

Around The Corporate Campfire

By Evelyn Clark

"Clark presents lessons on one of the executive's paramount responsibilities—communication—wrapped in some of America's best business stories. A 'must read.'"

Robert C. Wallace, CEO, Wallace Properties, Inc.

"With clarity and conciseness, Evelyn Clark provides graphic and compelling evidence of values-based storytelling and its role in building and sustaining a culture of success. This book serves as a practical guide for executives and managers of small or large organizations, public or private, nonprofit or for-profit. Examples of stories "around the corporate campfire" are drawn from a variety of organizations that meet the challenge of breathing life into organizational values. Clark tackles the essence of leadership and brings us a resource that will inspire and energize."

Roy Savoian, Dean, College of Business, Central Washington University

"Parables of success and failure always have been among the most important ways that learning is handed from generation to generation. This book is useful as its own parable for anyone who leads or aspires to lead."

***Burl Osborne, Chairman, The Associated Press and The Belo Foundation, Publisher Emeritus,* The Dallas Morning News**

"*Around the Corporate Campfire* is my favorite kind of book: intelligent, insightful and practical. It will make you a better storyteller and, in the process, a better communicator and leader. I recommend it."

Mark Sanborn, President, Sanborn & Associates, Inc., an idea studio for leadership development; Author, **The Fred Factor: How to Make Every Moment Extraordinary**

"In today's business driven world, it's easy to forget that any transaction comes down to people connecting with people. And stories connect in the most personal and intimate way possible. Evelyn Clark captures the essence of this idea and proves it powerfully, with stories, in *Around the Corporate Campfire*."

Ted Leonhardt, President, Anthem Group

"In *Around The Corporate Campfire*, we learn the story of many of the great names in business—Nike, Costco, Kodak, Southwest Airlines—to name just a few of the companies covered. Evelyn Clark provides many insights on the role of storytelling in communicating who these companies really are."

Steve Denning, Author, **The Springboard** *and* **The Squirrel,** *Former Program Director of Knowledge Management, World Bank*

"Evelyn Clark eloquently proves the rightful and important impact storytelling has in our culture. Through retold myths and tales, cultures are defined and passed down—an idea Clark summarily explains and justifies."

Doug Walker, Chairman and CEO, WRQ, Inc.

"Storytelling is the oldest form of record keeping, advertising, and tradition. Nothing surpasses a good story for the purpose of engaging the hearts and minds of people. Evelyn Clark helps us all take full advantage of the power, persuasion, and comfort of a really good story!"

Doug Lawrence, Minister of Worship, Menlo Park Presbyterian Church

"Around the Corporate Campfire stunningly documents a basic human need to know that each life has meaning as revealed through one's story and being part of a cultural/organizational story that is larger than oneself."

Jim and Linda Henry, Authors, **The Soul of the Physician, Doctors Speaking about Passion, Resilience and Hope**

"This wonderful book will show you how to get your message across to customers and employees through the time-tested, compelling, yet frequently ignored, medium of storytelling."

Dr. Patt Schwab, CSP, President, FUNdamentally Speaking, Author, **The Rubber Chicken Guide to Management**

"An interesting and helpful book. One can use these ideas with any size company. Everyone understands a story. It is not academic or hypothetical. It is the real world. Everyone understands the hero, his problems, and the outcome of his decisions. The bedrock of corporate culture is built by employees hearing the stories and identifying with the values in them."

Warren Van Genderen, Entrepreneur, Corporate Director

"At Kodak, corporate storytelling is essential. Businesses built on innovation often hearken back to their beginnings for inspiration and renewed creativity. Kodak founder George Eastman's legendary gift for bringing simplicity and convenience to picture taking continues to serve as a guidepost for the digital products we bring to our customers today."

David Kassnoff, Manager, Communications & Public Relations, Eastman Kodak Company

"Discover stories for a second time—once as a child, and now as a leader. Great leaders have told stories throughout the centuries. Why? Because storytelling, is ageless!! This book is ageless and should be kept in clear view to inspire you. The greatest storyteller was once a beginner. This book, I mean storybook, will help you on your journey towards great leadership."

David M. Armstrong, CEO, Armstrong International, Inc., Author, Managing by Storying Around

"I wish this book had been available during my years in management because it would have helped me communicate my vision and core values more effectively. Evelyn is a very gifted writer and obviously has a passion for using storytelling to promote core values throughout an organization. Anyone in a leadership position should learn to use stories."

Gary King, President and CEO (retired), Swanson Dean Corporation

"The stories told in an organization, formally and informally, shape the culture and define the environment. Evelyn Clark provides leaders with insights into telling stories that can bring mission statements and strategies to life, engaging employees and bringing out their full potential and passion for their work. We all want to tell meaningful stories about what we do every day, and Evelyn Clark helps us learn how."

Paul Erdahl, Vice President, Executive and Leadership Development, Medtronic

"It seems rather ironic that I spend many hours a day working with complex technologies and powerful tools to help people communicate. Yet, the simple, compelling story conveys information which technology, in and of itself, cannot create. Evelyn has written a book for anyone who works with people. This book relates what stories mean to a company—and what it means to departments and teams to have their own story. Realizing how others have used stories to reduce complexity and create momentum for their company is valuable and inspirational."

Scott Burbank, Director of Operations, Mobile and Embedded Device Division, Microsoft

"Stories are vibrant forms of expression that bring life and meaning to every human activity. Evelyn's book is an engaging probe into the art of storytelling, and anyone who wants to be a better communicator should read it."

Nelson Farris, Director of Education and Chief Storyteller, Nike

Around THE Corporate Campfire

Published by Insight Publishing Company
P.O. Box 4189
Sevierville, Tennessee 37864

10 9 8 7 6 5 4 3 2

ISBN 1-932863-04-4

Around THE Corporate Campfire

How Great Leaders Use Stories To Inspire Success

EVELYN CLARK

On The Cover

A mythical figure who has "spoken" to people for centuries, the flute player on the cover has become a popular image in modern culture, too, often seen in jewelry and gift items. Most commonly known as Kokopelli, he's an icon of the Pueblo Hopi people. Prolific on petroglyphs and pictographs throughout the Four Corners region of the American Southwest, Kokopelli's image is found as far away as Mexico and the California desert. An entertainer, fertility symbol, and mischief maker, he's incorporated in the author's business logo and Corporate Storytelling® trademark because he's also a mythical storyteller.

Did he evolve as a whimsical symbol of the Pueblo culture? Or was he a real person? Did he actually travel from village to village, entertaining with his flute by day and stories at night? No one knows. But historians agree that he was a very important symbol to the ancient Pueblo and related tribes.

To Gary, who has enriched the story
of my life immeasurably.

Table Of Contents

Acknowledgements

I will always owe a debt to an especially generous, gracious and brilliant management consultant based in Seattle by the name of David Dunning, PhD. It was David who pulled me up and dusted me off when I was experiencing career burnout. As he writes in the Foreword, he led me through the process of discovering my deep passion for aligning organizational behavior with corporate values, and he hung a new frame on my professional identity: The Corporate Storyteller.

I am grateful to countless others who have helped me, prodded me, advised me, taught me, and laughed with me throughout the process of creating and continually refining the Corporate Storytelling® workshop, developing a company-wide Corporate Storytelling system, and most recently, giving birth to this book. Foremost among those who served up insightful counsel with the right touch of humor were my patient, kind, and supportive husband, Gary Bequette; clinical psychologist, speaker/trainer, mediator, and friend Wally Wilkins, PhD; and speaker, recovering CFO, and friend Ron Rael, CPA. Other colleagues who generously offered book editing and authoring advice were Leslie Charles, Ann Hartley, and Dick Schaaf.

Dear friends who have offered unflagging support and encouragement include fashion designer and retailer Nubia Penuela Ryan; actress, artist, and coach Connie Miller; speaker and creativity consultant Marilyn Schoeman Dow; and the members of my study group from church: Susan Burbank, Linda Enkema, and Kathy Hitchcock.

Special mention goes to my former client and friend of 20 years, award-winning corporate communication manager Bonnie Bowman Henson, who assisted with both the research and the manuscript. Kay duPont served as chief editor, offering invaluable help with title development, content refinement, cover design, layout, and the countless details of syntax and punctuation. San Francisco newspaper columnist Dave Murphy also contributed editing guidance, particularly on the Introduction, as did Seattle-based newspaper columnist Eric Zoeckler. Mary Kay Van Sistine created the index, and graphics designer Kristin Adams applied her considerable talents to the cover art and text layouts.

Blessings to you all.

Foreword

What does a person do when asked to write a foreword for a book about Corporate Storytelling? That's easy! You begin by telling a story. All right, I will.

A few years ago I received a call from a woman whom I had met during a leadership consultation. I remembered her as being bright, articulate and energetic. She explained that she wanted to talk with me about some career issues she was confronting and explore some new directions. As we talked later in my office in downtown Seattle, she related coming through and surviving two tough life transitions but feeling dead ended in her present position in corporate public relations. I asked her to describe her frustration with her present work. That question hit a huge nerve. She jumped to her feet, clenched her fists, and looked me in the eye and shouted, "I'm sick of it! I'm sick of it! I don't want to be a corporate flack anymore!" I shot back and said, "Reframe it!" She came back and asked, "What do you mean?" I responded, "Reframe it. Be a Corporate Storyteller!" As the saying goes, The rest is history.

That afternoon Evelyn Clark began her journey to become one of the nation's leading Corporate Storytellers. This book, *Around the Corporate Campfire: How Great Leaders Use Stories to Inspire Success,* is about the power of stories in organizations today. We will learn how effective leaders use them in their organizations, and we will also learn how to successfully capture our corporate story and harness its power and energy.

Stories play a major therapeutic role in life. As earthly sojourners in the 21st century we experience the outer world in society, organizations and communities as paradoxical, rapidly changing, and becoming more globally inter-dependent. This outer world many times is at variance with our own inner world. And this is the therapeutic power of storytelling. Authentic storytelling provides us with meaning, understanding, and coping behaviors to successfully deal with the variance of the two worlds in which we live.

From a psychological standpoint we may agree that stories help us reconcile the outer and inner world contradictions that we face in our everyday life, but is there any quantitative evidence validating the efficacy of storytelling in corporate life?

Yes, there is solid evidence. Three research projects have found that storytelling is the bedrock of informal learning (see Appendix A). A six-year study conducted by The Center for Workforce Development examined the question, "Where does essential learning happen in the workplace?" An ambitious and comprehensive undertaking, the project partnered major corporations such as Boeing, Data Instruments, Motorola, and Siemens with their counterpart state agencies relating to corporate employment. The researchers found that *up to 70% of the new skills, information and competence in the workplace is acquired through informal learning.*

In another study Seely Brown describes the research of an anthropologist studying a service organization. The researcher found that essential job skill knowledge was transmitted informally among technical representatives around the coffee pot and during lunch through storytelling rather than in the training classroom.

Finally, Kleiner and Roth cite four reasons why storytelling is effective in organizations, and I have seen these validated over the years in my work with companies. In summary, stories build trust, are effective at raising hidden issues, have proved successful at transferring knowledge, and help build a body of generalizable knowledge about a corporation's management and leadership.

The philosopher George Santayana observed, "Those who cannot remember the past are condemned to repeat it." Stories throughout human history have helped us not only to avoid repeating the past, but to learn valuable lessons from it. So let's now step to the campfire and learn how leaders in the ensuing pages have used storytelling to build and strengthen their organizations.

David Dunning, PhD
Corporate Leadership Psychologist

Introduction

Nike employees have heard for years that their company owes its existence to a track coach and a waffle iron. Workers at Armstrong International know a round of golf once cost their CEO $248,000. And employees at Medtronic are brought to tears when they hear about a man with Parkinson's disease whose life was transformed by their company's technology.

Great leaders know that workers need more than lofty mission statements and industry buzzwords. To understand and appreciate what their organization stands for, workers need to hear about its people, its values, and its history. So smart leaders tell stories. And they periodically gather the "tribe" around the corporate campfire (the boardroom, annual meeting, holiday events, etc.) to recall the legends and share new tales. By touching the hearts as well as the minds of their employees, customers, and stakeholders, they leave a legacy of experiences that inspire generations.

"All you can do is relate the successful experiences you've had within the company," says Jim Sinegal, cofounder, President and CEO of Costco Wholesale. "What else have we *got* besides stories? That's what really hits home with people; it's what brings meaning to the work we do. And when you have real examples, like our success in selling Calvin Klein jeans, that's what resonates. A picture is worth a thousand words, and a story told appropriately is priceless. Telling one of our own stories speaks volumes about our philosophy and our values."

As the Costco story and others in this book demonstrate, the companies that last are the ones with visionary leaders who clearly articulate the organization's values—the bedrock of the corporate culture. Storytelling is a proven tool for reinforcing vision and values, and for communicating the practices and behaviors that lead to success. A consistently well-told corporate legend is the common thread among companies that succeed over time, diverse though their products and services may be.

Stories help us achieve a myriad of communication goals. And because they touch us deeply, they stay with us. Each time we share a story, we expand, deepen, and enhance our connections with our families, friends, communities, and organizations.

The Need for High Touch

We need stronger connections today, perhaps more than ever before. Our highly mobile, fast-moving, technology-driven culture gives us instant and continuous access to each other, but we're often not truly connected. Instead of speaking face-to-face, coworkers in nearby cubicles, next-door neighbors, and often even family and friends, opt for the greater efficiency of email or instant messages. But these "conveniences" isolate us from one another.

Telecommuting and home-based businesses add to our isolation because growing numbers of us have no one to interact with. Even in offices filled with people, we are so busy that the daily rituals of our past—sharing a coffee break, chatting at the water cooler, taking a few minutes to greet each other before a meeting—have been lost. Joseph Campbell reminds us in *The Power of Myth*, "When you lose rituals, you lose a sense of civilization; that's why our society is so out of kilter."

As Judy Wicks, founder, President, and maitre d' of Philadelphia's White Dog Café, so eloquently says, "People in our society hunger…to share their values, to enjoy a sense of community, and to be part of something that is larger than themselves."

Work Teams as Families

Given our common longing for increased connection, coworkers, managers, and even organizations themselves have become our "extended family." Leaders who regularly use stories create a culture in which people feel connected with other members of the "family," and that gives their employees' work purpose.

When executives and managers share tales about their own career challenges and failures, or relate how the company survived a crisis, overwhelmed employees take hope that they will also be able to tough it out. When leaders tell their teams how others have succeeded in solving difficult problems, employees gain confidence and motivation to carry on. An example of someone "caught doing something right" is easy to grasp and easy to apply. When desired behaviors and individual roles are clear, people work together better and serve customers more effectively.

Stories as Leadership Tools

Great leaders, teachers, and public speakers have long recognized the power of storytelling. Two thousand years ago, Jesus told parables that were so universal in their meaning and appeal they are still relevant today. We all know the stories of the Good Samaritan, the Prodigal Son, and the Lost Sheep. President John F. Kennedy mobilized an entire nation to put a man on the moon and return him safely to Earth by painting a picture through storytelling—not of what we were at the time, but of what we could become. Howard Goddard, PhD, former head of the English Department at Swarthmore College, taught, "The destiny of the world is determined less by the battles that are lost and won than by the stories it loves and believes in."

Top motivational speakers also recognize the power of stories to help them make a lasting impression. Grady Jim Robinson, a masterful keynote speaker who has earned the highest designations from the National Speakers Association, shares stories of his childhood. Even rowdy convention-goers expecting risqué entertainment come quickly to attention when Grady Jim starts talking about his father's tough-as-nails approach to parenting. Businesspeople often find themselves wiping away tears when he relates his doomed attempts to become the star baseball player his father expected him to be. Everyone can relate to his experience: trying your best but failing, disappointing someone you want to please, feeling worthless. Grady Jim delivers his message by taking his audiences through the experience. He holds their attention every second, and his message is far more effective as a result. The story stays with them.

The practice of storytelling in business has been spreading in recent years, and it's a long-standing tradition at the Harvard Business School. The school's highly respected case-study approach to preparing future leaders for the corporate world is essentially storytelling. Case studies start by describing a familiar scenario, set in a hypothetical company, and then discussing optional courses of action for the manager, weighing the pros and cons of each approach. Caught up in the story, students immediately begin working on their own plans, hoping to come up with the recommended solution—or something better.

Values Shared through Stories

In our cynical world, the word *story* is often considered synonymous with *fabrication*, but that's erroneous. Stories are the way we usually communicate. "How's your day going?" "What's the status of your project?" "What's the latest on the company's new product?" Each of these everyday questions is often answered in story form, although most people don't think of themselves as storytellers.

Business leaders need to clearly and passionately communicate their organization's values and vision so they can draw everyone into the fold: prospective recruits, employees, customers, stockholders, associates, suppliers, and other "corporate family" stakeholders. One of the most effective communication tools is storytelling. A leader who is able to identify and develop an authentic corporate story and tell it effectively is similar to a masterful conductor who leads an orchestra through the most challenging musical arrangement. The storytelling leader is able to get everyone to "play the same song," to understand and identify the corporate values, and to enact those values as part of their daily responsibilities.

Southwest Airlines (see page 147) is a prime example of using stories to generate growth. The founders' vision has been clear to everyone in the organization since 1971, when cofounders Herb Kelleher and Rollin King launched the company on the core values of no frills and a lot of fun. The focus of corporate communications has been to convey those values through the Southwest story—in advertising, in employee messages, in news articles, and on the Web site. Disproving the traditional belief that fun and laughter are inappropriate in the serious realm of business, Southwest has created a level of employee loyalty that few can rival. And throughout periods of economic turmoil in the economy and a steady procession of corporate scandals and bankruptcies,

Southwest has been the only U.S.-based airline to consistently show a profit.

Successful Leaders as Storytellers

In the following chapters, you will learn how a number of top organizations have put their hearts and souls into their stories to achieve their goals—in management, in training, and sometimes even in advertising.

"Companies will thrive on the basis of their stories and myths—on their ability to create products and services that evoke emotion," futurist Rolf Jensen predicts. After reading the stories in this collection, you'll agree that we have entered a new phase in business management—an era in which leaders are becoming the caretakers of the organization's history as well as its future.

So as you read the corporate legends on the following pages, ask yourself: Is our organization honoring its legends? Are we touching people's minds *and hearts*? Are we sharing the stories that will create the future we most desire?

Now, pull up a chair, imagine yourself warming up to a campfire, and turn the page. The first tale is about to begin.

1

Armstrong International: Mastering The Art Of Storying Around

After attending Alma College, David Armstrong entered the business world and felt compelled to change his management approach every two or three years to follow the latest trend: Management by Objectives, X Theory, Y Theory, the One-Minute Manager, to name just a few. But once he discovered storytelling, he never even considered trying anything else.

Inspired during his pastor's sermon one Sunday in the 1980s, Armstrong was struck by the fact that everyone—even people who had been nodding off—sat up straight and began listening attentively when the preacher launched into a story. Why wouldn't stories command attention in a business setting too, he wondered. As he weighed the possibility, he realized that people of every age and every culture love to hear a good story. So he decided to try storytelling to communicate corporate values and honor employee successes at Armstrong International, where he's now Chief Executive Officer. Once he did, he was hooked.

"There's no way I, or anyone else, could ever outlive storytelling," he says. "It's been around for thousands of years. The greatest leaders of all time have used stories, including Abraham Lincoln, Jesus, and even Attila the Hun. Whether you like their leadership or what they did, that's how they led. And each one was very effective in accomplishing his goals."

Armstrong is a master of not only telling effective stories, but also of creating titles that grab attention. His first book features stories such as "Go Directly to Jail—and Collect $200," "Bozo Cancer," "The $1.2-Million Maintenance Man," and "Shut Up and Eat Your M&Ms." Armstrong's personal favorite from the first collection is "Leaders Make Mistakes, Too."

That story is about a customer order that required intricate welding on copper coils. When the welding shop completed the job, it was clear that the product was not up to Armstrong International's standards; the welding would almost certainly break in time. The choice: scrap a job that had cost $2,000 in materials, plus labor, and recoup only $300 by selling it as parts; or try to salvage the job by grinding away the weak welds and redoing them.

The general foreman of the work team, Chuck Rockwell, needed to pick up Armstrong at the airport, so he left the decision to his foreman. The foreman discussed the situation with his welding team, and they agreed it would be better to start over.

When Armstrong and Rockwell returned to the plant and learned of the decision, Rockwell confessed to Armstrong in front of everyone, "It's my fault we had this problem. I knew that welding copper is extremely difficult, but I didn't spend enough time with either our foreman or our welders to show them what needed to be done."

Then Rockwell sold the scrap. But he didn't put the $300 back into his available budget. Instead, he threw a party! He figured that if he celebrated his mistake, everyone would learn from the experience and remember the lessons. They would learn how to weld copper, and they would learn that even bosses make mistakes.

Armstrong loves that story because it helps people feel safe about taking risks and making mistakes without the fear of being fired. "People think bosses don't make mistakes. I think they believe that because that's what bosses tell them!" Armstrong muses. "To me, it's so powerful when you learn that a leader really means what he said. And the fact that the boss' boss' boss wrote a story about it told people, 'It's OK.'

"Far more independent decisions are being made in that department now. Talk is cheap. But when someone throws a party to celebrate a mistake, that sends a powerful message."

Armstrong follows that story with the comment that supporting failure does not mean supporting sloppiness. Rather, he points out, failure is good only when something is learned from it and the idea is quickly modified. He also repeats management guru Tom Peters' lesson that failing is not enough; you must fail big. Armstrong adds, "Significant gains come from significant risks."

Peters has had a strong influence on Armstrong, even creating the title for the first of Armstrong's books, *Management by Storying Around.* And that's an interesting story in itself.

"Any new and bold and different idea has difficulty getting accepted," Armstrong says, "so people thought I was wacko when I started telling stories around the factory floor." He persevered, though, and when he enrolled in Tom Peters' Skunk Camp, one of the assignments was to go back to the office, work on a report about the techniques they were using to run their companies, and return several weeks later with three of their top executives. The executive group from each company would then deliver their presentation to the class.

To say that Armstrong's group lacked confidence in their presentation would be a prime example of understatement. Their concern grew exponentially as other groups gave their reports. Some of the reports were slick audiovisual productions.

Others enacted their presentations in full theatrical costumes. All were elaborate. Already embarrassed by the humiliation ahead, the Armstrong International team slumped down in their chairs when their company's name was called. Their presentation was plain vanilla in a room of fanciful flavors, and they were certain they were licked before they started. The storytelling CEO walked alone to the front of the room and told four stories. That was it. No performance, no music, no pictures, no passing of the baton. Just Armstrong telling a few tales of people caught doing things right.

When he finished, the room erupted. Questions started flying. How long had Armstrong being using stories? How did he decide which ones to tell? How did he learn about extraordinary customer service or risky decision-making? What made him think that celebrating failure would be effective? Wasn't that counter to what every respected business school taught? The discussion went on and on, and Peters saw that Armstrong was onto something. When Armstrong noticed that Peters was scribbling away on his notepad, he became concerned. He thought Peters was going to skewer him for the simple presentation about his simple approach to management.

Instead, Peters was excited. Armstrong's fresh way of using the ancient communication device of storytelling was intriguing. He urged Armstrong to publish a collection of his stories as a business book and handed him a page of doodles, which included the title that came to him as he listened to Armstrong's presentation. Two days later a publisher called, and shortly thereafter *The New York Times* wrote an article about Armstrong's unique leadership method. Calls followed from businesspeople around the U.S. and around the world.

Doubleday published the first edition in hardcover, and Armstrong International published the paperback and three succeeding books, *How to Turn Your Company's Parables into*

Profit; Once Told, They're Gold; and *Chief Storytelling Officer*. Now the company offers all three books and several videos for sale online. "Storytelling is a great style of communication," Armstrong says, "and as you use it, you just keep getting better."

Among those that stand out as favorites is "The Day I Paid $248,000 to Play a Round of Golf." As you might expect, this isn't about greens fees! Here's what happened:

While Armstrong was enjoying a morning away from the office, the assistant general manager of the Florida plant bought two machines for a total cost of—no surprise here—$248,000. That may not seem unusual, but the catch is that Jerry Gilchrist's spending authority was only $20,000! We can all imagine how most CEOs would react after discovering that an employee had exceeded his spending limit more than 12 times over. But in this case, the manager wasn't fired. In fact, his decision was celebrated, and Gilchrist was honored by having his story selected for inclusion in one of the books.

Why in the world would an executive honor an employee for ignoring the limits on his own authority? The answer is simple. Gilchrist had the opportunity to get a fantastic deal on equipment the company planned to buy within a few months anyway. When a supplier suddenly offered two barely-used machines for sale at an extremely attractive price, and someone else also was interested, Gilchrist decided to jump at the great price, saving the company a significant amount of money in the long run. Also, having the equipment on hand sooner enabled them to catch up on a backlog of orders. The results: Armstrong International was able to reap significant savings, provide better customer service, and demonstrate its commitment to employee risk-taking. And Armstrong was truly happy to pay $248,000 in exchange for a morning on the golf course.

A fourth-generation family-owned company headquartered in Michigan, Armstrong international has locations in the U.S., Europe, the Far East, and Canada and describes itself as one of the most unique manufacturing companies in the world. Maker of steam-system equipment and provider of steam-consulting services, the company doesn't resemble a typical factory. The CEO believes in creating an atmosphere where people have fun, as evidenced by his approval of the party to celebrate Gilchrist's "mistake." Additional evidence: the company's parking-lot stripes appear to be drawn with crayons, and the stalls reserved for disabled drivers show the familiar wheelchair symbol with balloons attached. When visitors sign in at the reception counter, the writing instruments provided are...you guessed it...crayons! On-site transportation is provided by golf carts painted to resemble animals known for their speed, and conference rooms are decorated in playful themes. One is painted to look like a sports stadium, and it's carpeted in Astroturf®.

Set on establishing the short story as the literature trademark of corporate America, Armstrong threw away policy and procedures manuals and instead began writing stories of "people caught doing something right." He writes the stories longhand, frames them, and presents them to the individual featured. The framed vignettes decorate walls of employees' homes and work spaces around the company. Initially Armstrong compiled the stories every six months into a simply-bound collection and circulated the "book" throughout the company. The compilations were an immediate hit; employees checked them out overnight so they could read all the stories right away. They wanted to see if they or any of their own team members were featured. The original intent was to distribute the story collections only to employees so they could learn "the Armstrong way" of conducting business, and that practice continues. But as word of Armstrong's innovative approach to management spreads around the business world and Armstrong delivers more and more keynote speeches on his technique, he continually finds additional uses for the stories.

"You can't forget the culture as you grow; it's very hard to keep alive," he points out. "But stories are helping me do it, and they've been very effective. You can address any issue through stories."

Observing that most companies hiring management consultants have lost the essence of their cultures, Armstrong says, "To keep our culture alive, I post stories on bulletin boards, I put them in paycheck envelopes, and we've framed some to hang on the walls as decorations. We've recorded stories on CD to allow our salespeople to listen to them in their cars, and we've recorded several videotapes that we play on TV sets installed in the factories. A lot of people wanted to reenact their own stories, and everybody enjoys watching a 3-4-minute story. Television is a great way to communicate because it's user friendly and familiar."

The company also scatters copies of the books around its facilities, including the reception areas, so employees and visitors alike can enjoy reading a story or two while waiting for a meeting to start. Armstrong also uses the books when recruiting employees. He asks candidates to take a book home and read it to learn about the corporate culture and determine whether it's the kind of place they would like to work. He asks engineers to read stories about innovation and tell him what they think about the company's practices.

How does he know his effectiveness as a manager and a communicator is due to the use of stories? Armstrong says that he hasn't conducted any formal benchmark studies because "observation is enough. Our turnover is extremely low, even during volatile times. People like what I talk about, such as the importance of having fun at work. I can let everyone in the company see what I want by distributing these stories many different ways, and sooner or later they'll hear the message. That helps keep people here. They start living the stories and bragging about them. They even give our books as gifts to their friends and relatives!"

Armstrong believes that a leader who stays close to the details of operations is able to stay on top of what's going on. "I know of cases where stories have helped us manage our health care plan. And we're able to control expense account spending because people remember a story about our travel policy. We expect them to live on the road the way they do at home, and they're careful to honor that because it allows for individual preferences rather than a forced standard.

"The powerful stories are in the details of these issues. The details speak loudly and provide strong evidence of whether you mean what you say."

Although the privately-held company doesn't disclose financial information, Armstrong says, "Our income statements and monthly financials reflect that we're very profitable. That's all the proof I need. When I step outside my office door, I feel, see, and experience the difference that storytelling makes. I don't need to try anything else. Storytelling works!"

For more information on the Armstrong story, go to www.armstrongstories.com.

2

Nike:
A Global Competitor Running On Waffle Soles

When the waffles on a track coach's breakfast plate look like great running shoes, there's only one thing for him to do: jump up from the table, sprint to the garage, and pour latex on his wife's waffle iron. When that impulse leads him to develop a better, lighter outer sole for his team, the gratification more than compensates for a ruined waffle iron and, at least temporarily, a miffed wife. Those hurdles were easy to clear because, as employees of Nike, Inc., and many sports devotees know, that man was the University of Oregon's Bill Bowerman. He had just taken the first steps toward cofounding Nike and launching the worldwide jogging craze.

Cofounder, Chairman, and CEO Phil Knight, an accounting student who was a middle-distance runner on Bowerman's 1957 team, has run the business nearly from the beginning and owns over 30% of the company. But Nike's collective soul is based on Bowerman's philosophies, which have lived on after his death at the end of 1999.

Bowerman's mission was "to bring inspiration and innovation to every athlete in the world," and he always insisted that "if you have a body, you are an athlete." He also taught his athletes to seek the competitive edge—not only in their bodies, but in their gear and their passion. Understanding this heritage is intrinsic to Nike's corporate culture, according to Nelson Farris, Director of Education and Chief Storyteller. Virtually nothing at Nike is formal, including the leaders' approach to using vignettes to motivate and communicate. "It's what we've done from the beginning," Farris says. "If you've got a high-energy company where people are excited about what they're doing, you tell stories about what happened today, yesterday, an hour ago. It reinforces our 'Just do it' attitude.

"If we connect people with our heritage and give them freedom to excel, chances are they won't view Nike as just another place to work. We think of this as internal branding—stories about people getting things done."

According to a story told in Northwest business circles, the enduring line "Just do it" became the core of Nike's advertising program when an ad agency executive noticed that Knight often used those words. Demonstrating implicit trust in his management team's abilities, Knight swept aside any notions of an elaborate approval process. Instead, as the agency exec noted, whenever managers asked for his feedback on their plans, Knight would simply say, "Just do it!" Farris neither confirms nor denies the validity of the story, acknowledging that, whether or not it's based on fact, it's a compelling legend that captures the spirit of the organization, and it also hit a bull's eye with the original target market. People who buy Nike products aren't couch-potato spectators; they're active people who go out and just do it.

Nike's mission is to inspire these everyday athletes and to deliver innovative products that will keep them going. More than just an advertising campaign with a catchy call to action that became a slogan, "Just do it" is a corporate mantra, a Nike way of doing business. The staying power of the Nike brand is solid proof that the company has been on the right track from the beginning. Nike owns 40% of the U.S. athletic shoe market and is a major player in 140 other countries. The company's facilities are spread from world headquarters in Oregon to European headquarters in The Netherlands. Nike also operates leased facilities for 15 NikeTowns, over 70 Nike Factory Stores, two NIKEgoddess boutiques, and over 100 sales and administrative offices. Global sales for all products combined totaled $10.7 billion in fiscal year 2003, up 8% from the year before, and sales outside the U.S. surpassed home-based numbers for the first time. At the end of 2003, worldwide futures orders were up 9.7% over the same period the previous year.

Befitting its casual, sports-based culture, Nike has always given storytelling a central role in the company's communications, from the corporate Web site to employee communications to the annual report. And the storytelling approach has been effective both internally and externally. Of course it helps that Nike's target markets—both professional athletes and active, sports-oriented people—are by nature story-rich environments where athletes create dramatic stories through their performances. "We're one of the few businesses where you can go home, turn on the TV, and see stories about people using what you worked on today," Farris points out.

The leading sports and fitness company in the world also has one of the lowest employee turnover rate in the industry. Not only the 4,000 at world headquarters in Beaverton, Oregon, but approximately 23,000 employees around the world are familiar with the Nike legend and understand their role in maintaining the top spot. New employees at corporate headquarters spend two full days in orientation sessions, which may include a trip to the nearby University of Oregon track where Bowerman trained his teams. They also take a tour of the corporate heritage museum, which displays the now-famous waffle iron and other corporate and sports memorabilia. "People come in here, they like the place, they appreciate the freedom," Farris explains. "I always tell them, 'If we didn't want you, why did we hire you? If you want to succeed, step right up.

The opportunities here are open.' The ones who understand it will get right to it." According to a *Bloomberg News* article, many "ekins" (Nike spelled backwards), as select field tech reps are called, are so loyal to the company and their CEO that they have the Nike "swoosh" tattooed on their legs and shoulders. Knight himself has a swoosh on his ankle.

"We tell stories all the time about everything around here...about the evolution and heritage," Farris says. "Around the product, we have stories, too. There are also great stories about our athletes, which we share with employees. We do a lot of in-house videos, and when people start complaining, we can show them the Lance Armstrong story and tell them 'Get over it; you can survive with the number of pencils you have,' or whatever they were complaining about!"

As *Fast Company* magazine pointed out in "The Nike Story: Just Tell It," a January 2000 article on Nike's deliberate use of storytelling as a leadership tool, Nike realizes that "the stories you tell about your past shape your future." The company's senior executives are designated "corporate storytellers," which means they are responsible for "explaining their company's heritage to everyone from vice presidents and sales reps to the hourly workers who run the cash registers at Nike's stores," according to the magazine.

Now more than ever, Nike sees its job as bringing innovation to the great sweating masses to expand their potential, no matter their skill level. That's why the company's story-based advertising not only shines the spotlight on exceptional sports figures, but also on recreational athletes, including the growing numbers of women in professional and amateur sports. In 2001, after soliciting input from prospective female customers for 18 months, Nike launched a women's line of innovative athletic gear, a Web site (www.nikegoddess.com) with a magazine format, and NikeGO, a program focused on motivating girls aged 8-15 to become active, partly by giving them the means to do it. In the first year of the new line, total combined men's and women's apparel revenues reached nearly $300,000, and by the end of FY2003 were $2.5 billion and growing.

Ginny Turner represents a portion of the market Nike wants to reach. A 46-year-old grandmother and Nike employee, she adopted an active lifestyle. She began by losing 100 pounds in nine months through exercise and healthy eating. Then she completed marathons and ultra-marathons in 44 states and five continents, raising thousands of dollars for charities along the way. The company was so impressed that Turner's story was told on the corporate Web site to inspire others.

Many similar stories of employee involvement are told online. The company actively encourages employees to get involved in charitable activities and then shares the "social profits" with everyone. For example, in 2001, FedEx and Nike teamed up to ship more than 12,000 new clothing items and 6,000 baseball caps to India's earthquake victims. That same week, the Nike/FedEx team transported about two tons of relief materials, including 10,586 warmup suits, to El Salvador quake victims. And after the September 11, 2001, attack on New York's World Trade Center, Nike stepped up to the fundraising/giving challenge and bolted out of the blocks early. In a seven-week, 3,431-mile run from the West Coast town of Astoria, Oregon, to New York City, 265 Nike employees honored America's firefighters and their families and raised more than $2.6 million.

Concern for community extends to concern for the environment. In September 1995, Knight heard Paul Hawken, author of *The Ecology of Commerce*, speak at a conference, and Hawken's words led to an epiphany. As Knight summed it up,

"The planet's living systems are in decline; without them, there is no such thing as society, let alone business." Not long after Hawken's speech, Nike's executive team added another key component to corporate goals: sustainability. Carrying out that commitment to sustainable business practices requires Nike to do its part to restore the environment and thereby help to ensure a good quality of life for the world's children and grandchildren.

"[We knew intuitively that] making decisions based on what is good for future generations will help create a company built to last," Knight wrote in the company's first *Corporate Responsibility Report* in 2001. Although sustainability became a new core value, the concept wasn't new at Nike. Nine years before, Nike's footwear chemical-engineering team, spearheaded by Dick Crosbie, developed water-based alternatives to petroleum-based adhesives, primers, degreasers, and mold-release agents. Since 1994, this new technology has led to an 88% reduction in the use of organic solvent by Nike's contract manufacturers. These reductions have also saved Nike several million dollars in raw materials since May 2000 and in many cases have improved factory environmental conditions for the approximately 660,000 contract factory workers making Nike-branded product throughout the world. Nike has even shared results and technical information with its competitors to increase the benefits of this technology worldwide.

Building on that early success, the company audited some of its suppliers and the materials they use, then focused specifically on the chemical components used in Nike products. In another move, Nike made a formal commitment in 2001 to reducing greenhouse gas emissions across its operations worldwide by establishing a partnership with the World Wildlife Fund (WWF) and the Center for Energy and Climate Solutions. Nike is also working to reduce emissions at its own office, manufacturing facilities and distribution centers. David B. Sandlow, Executive Vice President of the WWF, says, "Nike is making great strides in its effort to help save the planet.... It's simply good, smart corporate citizenship."

For several years, the company has worked to phase out the use of polyvinyl choloride (vinyl or PVC), which threaten workers' health as well as the environment. In partnership with a number of retailers and local recycling outlets, Nike also routinely collects and recycles one to two million pairs of footwear (of any brand) in the U.S. each year. More than 13 million pairs were processed from the beginning of the recycling program in 1993 through early 2003. One of the resulting products is trademarked as Nike Grind, a composite of rubber granules and other materials used to resurface playgrounds, basketball courts, and track and field surfaces. Another product, FieldTurf, is used as underlay on soccer fields.

In addition to Knight's heightened personal awareness about social responsibility, a major impetus for launching the 2001 *Corporate Responsibility Report* can be found in press reports that took the company to task over its alleged human-rights violations overseas. Being #1 in the sports field made Nike a natural punching bag, and Farris is quick to concede that the story blindsided the executive team.

The pummeling began in 1992 when an investigative reporter charged Nike with ignoring abysmal working conditions in its contract manufacturing facilities. Campus activists grabbed the global sweatshop banner and paraded it worldwide. Years of adverse publicity followed, including a lawsuit filed by an individual in California that resulted in an unfavorable ruling. While not addressing the merit of the allegations, the California Supreme Court ruled that, because a company's public statements about operations might persuade consumers to buy its products, those statements must be treated as commercial speech, thereby limiting constitutional protection. The Court agreed that public statements include those appearing in news stories, op-ed pieces, press releases, and Web sites—any published statement that would reach residents of California. Nike appealed to the U.S. Supreme Court, which in June 2003 dismissed the suit on technical grounds and returned the case to the California courts. Although the U.S. justices issued no formal decision, a majority rejected the central holding of the state court that Nike's speech at issue could be restricted as purely "commercial." The case has since been settled.

As Farris acknowledges, "Stories have a way of backfiring when you underestimate the power of the press and let someone tell the negative side before you have a chance to tell the positive side. We've learned the power of working with the press, and we make sure to have designated spokespersons who understand how to do that. We understand that we have a huge responsibility as the most powerful sports brand in the world, and that means we need to be better communicators with the outside world."

Fast Company pointed out in its report, "Through all of these ups and downs, winning companies hold on to their values." To which Farris added, "To survive those downtimes, you have to understand what real teamwork is—keeping promises, keeping commitments. Not everyone understood this, but that's what Bowerman taught his athletes."

Pushed by events and pulled by their own consciences, Nike has taken steps to improve contract factory working conditions and has ramped up monitoring efforts at the facilities. The company also has learned that labor problems—harassment, overtime issues, pay, safety, health—are thorny issues not easily resolved. The task is even more complex because Nike-branded products are made in more than 900 contract factories and more than 50 countries. In Vietnam, for example, Nike's contract factories constitute the largest private employer in the country, and exports of Nike products account for 6% of its total.

Addressing child labor is an ongoing, complex challenge. Nike's age standards are among the highest in the world, but next to impossible to verify in places like Cambodia and Bangladesh, where birth records are easily forged or don't exist. But, true to its commitment, Nike has taken responsibility for creating a good quality of life for its workers. The company, for example, contracts with eight centers in Pakistan, where several thousand workers have access to free lunches, a free medical clinic for the stitcher and family, a fair-price shop, day care, kindergarten, and a recreation center. Like putting the genie back in the bottle, the damage to the company's reputation is hard to undo. But Nike is committed to continuous improvement in working conditions and congruence in its corporate story.

"We were doing the right thing all along," Knight said in the 2001 *Corporate Responsibility Report*. "The biggest problem was that we didn't get in front of the labor issue…. Someone else saw with their eyes the negative side of that story rather than the positive side. The factories of the past were abysmal, the factories of the '90s are awesome; they'll be even better this decade. If there are problems, you fight through them. Our objective is to get the truth on the table; when you're wrong, fess up and fix up. That's the kind of attitude you have to have. You can't run any business being dishonest. It makes for great stories when you acknowledge you were wrong and correct it."

Farris adds, "In the past, Nike had no power, but when we got big enough, we could in some cases exert more muscle in the labor arena. High volume in some contract factories gave us clout to help factories with cultural, economic, and government issues. Now our suppliers are directed to meet high standards." As a percentage of the Western Hemisphere's $760 billion import/export market, Nike's $10.7 billion in fiscal 2003 sales still doesn't make it a 500-pound gorilla without the muscle of the Fair Labor Association (FLA), a coalition the company helped to form.

In the midst of demonstrating that human rights and good business practice can coexist, "Nike was growing like topsy and lost its focus, forgetting to be competitive," Knight said. In a three-year period, revenues more than tripled and the company found itself "understaffed, overworked, and euphoric." At the same time, "Asian economies melted down" and the company undertook a massive overhaul of its supply chain, which required three years to complete.

Taking responsibility for the company's fiscal 2001 performance, which he called "more gutsy than great," Knight focused on the finish of a 10-year plan for becoming a "truly global company." The immediate goal was to find capable additions to the management team to help the company fulfill its vision. That goal was accomplished the same year when Charlie Denson and Mark Parker were named copresidents of Nike Brand, and they are rising to the challenges, which included a lingering downturn in the U.S. economy. Over the previous five years, U.S. sales grew an average of just 1.6% a year.

As Farris described the company's situation, Nike's previous mission was to be the world's best sports and fitness company, and that goal has been reached. "Now we're the #1 brand with the most recognized corporate logo, so our old mission statement is no longer aspirational. Today we're re-energizing ourselves with what can be, rather than what is."

"Our world has become much bigger, our impact felt beyond sports," Knight wrote, pointing out that the company redrafted its mission and values to reflect this evolution and identify opportunities for growth, both as a business and as a global citizen. Nike boiled these values down to 11 "maxims," or fundamental truths, and they form the crux of every story told at the company these days. To paraphrase the maxims:

1. Innovation is Nike's nature.
2. Nike is a company.
3. Nike is a brand.
4. Simplify and go (chuck the old ways).
5. The consumer decides.
6. Be a sponge (constantly learn, evolve immediately, and don't dwell on a five-year business plan).
7. Evolve immediately (don't dwell on a five-year business plan, execute your ideas, then we'll reward them).
8. Do the right thing (for people, the environment, and socially).
9. Master the fundamentals.
10. Always be on the offense (play to win).
11. Remember "the man" (we all exist because of Bill Bowerman and what he put in motion is what we still are today).

"When you shift to a broader-based company, you need to weave these truths into the culture," Farris says, "and that takes some time. The best way is for senior leaders to walk the talk." To that end, Nike held a series of two-hour meetings with 5,000 employees in Beaverton, then with 1,000 in Europe. Then they conducted country-by-country gatherings with local people translating what the company's done and adjusting the message for cultural differences.

The stories executives repeat to employees reflect the broadening definition of sports. As Knight explained, although

Nike has always been about sports, the definition has grown a bit fuzzy, maybe even a little confining. "Yoga? Freestyling? Are they sports? They're all play, and play is the body's natural state...the root of every sport. The kid running to the swingset, the woman hugging the face of El Captain, the 75-year-old dancer.... Play is for everybody."

Knight's own play time still includes running and two other sports: tennis and golf, "depending on whether I want to abuse my elbow, my knees, or my emotions."

So much has changed since Bill Bowerman's inspired run to the garage. Nike has become the dominant world brand in sports and fitness and a global leader in doing what's right. And the Nike swoosh is one of the most recognized brands on earth. Through it all, the core values of inspiration and innovation have not wavered.

Any way you look at it, it's an impressive record in world competition for the runner from the University of Oregon. Bill Bowerman would be proud. And his words will not be forgotten, although his familiar quote has acquired a "footnote" on Nike's Web site: "If you have a body, you are an athlete. And as long as there are athletes, there will be Nike."

For more information on the Nike story, go to www.nikebiz.com.

3

3M:

Nurturing A Spiral Of Growth And Creativity

3M employees embrace the company's well-known and often-told stories with great enthusiasm. The stories help them form ideas about winning, see themselves more clearly, and explain their departmental and individual roles to one another.

Steve Webster, staff vice president of Six Sigma, says that 3M employees' penchant for storytelling started with legends about the company's first heroes. Now they power the 3M mindset.

One of 3M's earliest heroes was William L. McKnight. He rose steadily from bookkeeper in 1907 to President, a position he held for 20 years before being named Chairman of the Board in 1949. The legends surrounding his business philosophy and management style set the tone for a culture of employee inventiveness, career opportunities, and continuous growth.

In the firm belief that a destructively critical manager crushes creativity, McKnight pushed his managers to stand behind employees with the gumption to champion new ideas. He did concede, however, that his wasn't always the easiest path. "Managing such an enterprise takes considerable tolerance," he said. Still, he insisted that the "mistakes employees make, if they're essentially right about everything else, aren't as serious as mistakes management will make if it undertakes to tell those in authority exactly how they must do their jobs."

The idea incubator McKnight built at 3M continues to foster innovation. The company has many programs that encourage employees to take risks. The 15% Rule, for instance, allows employees to spend part of their work time exploring experiments, and "Acceleration" gives employees the chance to work on high-profile projects. This encouraging culture gives employees the freedom to try unorthodox theories—a hallmark of the stories 3M tells about itself. There's the story about the abject failure of their first abrasive products, the ones about inventing masking tape and Wetordry sandpaper, and the one about a 3M scientist's wish for a bookmark that wouldn't fall out of his hymnal leading to Post-it® Notes.

Managers' tolerance of small mistakes along the road to big discoveries has generated a steady stream of more than 50,000 products intended to make the world a better place.

The history of this $17-billion company is displayed in 3M's Innovation Center at its St. Paul, Minnesota, headquarters, where new employees and visitors alike get a flavor for the century-old company, its developments, its products, and its technologies. Exhibits play up photos and stories about some of the 67,000 employees whose work has made significant contributions to 3M's success.

"I make a point to spend time taking people through the Center's displays, so they get to know our story," explains Steve Webster. "When you see the broad portfolio of all our businesses in one room, it's clear what the connections are and why it all makes sense...a bit like getting to know the members of a family. Visitors' responses are universally positive. They're pretty impressed."

Considering that 3M's far-flung outposts in more than 60 nations serve customers in nearly 200 countries, Webster takes it as a special compliment when customers tell him 3M people are all the same. "In a corporation this large, we are fortunate to have many diverse employees, yet when our customers say we all behave the same—that we all speak with one voice on the important stuff—then we're definitely on the right track as a company."

Webster's talking about an environment where everyone reads from the same page—an environment he's proud to say permeates 3M. "When you ask people about 3M heroes or about our company's set of values, you unanimously get the right answers: '3M stands for innovation, new ideas for our customers and support of our people.' A company built on such a strong culture means people will do the right thing without being told."

Leaders reward "doing the right thing" verbally and in more tangible ways. A set of awards for heroic achievement reinforces the value that intelligent passion brings to the company. The Circle of Technical Excellence and Innovation Award recognizes exceptional individuals whose achievements set the standard for excellence worldwide and affirm that the corporate values stand together to build new business.

Nominees for membership in the Carlton Society—the most prestigious accolade given a 3M scientist—must have demonstrated technical excellence over an entire career. The evening of the induction ceremony honors winners, and at least half an hour of the three-hour event also focuses on details about the life and times of a former Carlton Society hero—perhaps a recent nominee, or maybe a winner from many years past.

Company-wide publicity also surrounds winners of the Golden Step award. It's given for putting a new product on the market that exceeds annual sales of $10 million and reaches profitability within three years of its launch. "Since we're here to grow the company, commercialize products, and invent new businesses, the Golden Step Award is the pinnacle of recognition at 3M," Webster says.

A number of these hero stories reside on a special section of the company Web site. The narratives illustrate how determination in the face of daunting challenges earned those highlighted the respect and admiration of their peers and supervisors. Many stories end with the heroes sharing a secret or two of their successes for the benefit of other innovators. Here are some examples: Mark Ellis pursued a bold hypothesis that scientists might be able to harness "runaway" chemical reactions, an idea crucial to his later development of a highly efficient process for manufacturing low-cost, solventless, pressure-sensitive adhesives. Ellis encourages other 3Mers to have fun with what they do: "That sense of fun becomes contagious and everyone does the job that much better. A sense of humor is also helpful. Innovation thrives on a positive outlook."

Bill Wood created the 3M Cubitron™ Abrasive Grain that one grateful customer called "the first truly new development in grinding wheels in 40 years." Ever on the lookout for the "next great thing," Wood says the shape of one of the foods he was recently served at a restaurant suggested a way to solve an abrasives problem he'd been laboring over for quite some time. "You never know when or where a good idea can emerge," he says.

Jim Onstott agrees that keeping an open, active mind at all times, even off the job, pays big dividends. During his career, he's earned seven patents and written numerous scientific papers about specialty optical fibers. He's earned a reputation as "Professor" Onstott, a mentor eager to help the people lined up outside his office door who are either seeking technical guidance or waiting to see if their insight is new to Onstott. "I rarely have a creative thought at work," he admits. "There are too many distractions." Most of his scientific breakthroughs come from letting his mind wander back to work while driving a tractor on his minifarm.

John Moon's story exemplifies the credibility a researcher must build among 3Mers to create a winning team. His affability, sense of humor, generosity of spirit, and roll-up-the-sleeves attitude over a long career have won his colleagues' respect and affection and created the team spirit necessary to drive a product to market. "Commercialization [of the pressure-sensitive-adhesive product under development] depended on production people and engineers meshing beautifully," Moon says. "We needed everybody—from the people in the trenches to the scientists from Central Research to supportive management—to get the job done."

Communication through story can be seen everywhere at 3M, not just in scientific pursuits. Trainers immerse sales representatives in company lore and teach them to paint word-picture anecdotes so customers can "see" how 3M products will help them succeed. Vignettes of both heroic and everyday innovations fill the pages of *The Stemwinder*, 3M's employee publication. And Gordon Shaw demonstrated before his retirement that storytelling can—and should—positively impact a corporation's administrative functions. He believes in story so much, in fact, that he and two colleagues wrote an article on the subject for a 1998 *Harvard Business Review*. But let him tell the story of how he became convinced of the necessity to add narrative to a strong strategic plan:

One day, as Shaw stared down at a business document formatted in the corporate world's standard presentation style of bulleted items, he wondered why the same storytelling principles that had proved effective in other facets of 3M operations couldn't also be applied to strategic planning.

It's true that bulleted lists are economical and save time, he reasoned, and they can also reduce complex business situations to simple concepts. Furthermore, presenting a list doesn't hamper discussion of issues peripheral to, but perhaps not essential to, the subject at hand. "But at what cost?" Shaw asked himself.

Since writing is thinking, and bullets allow people to bypass the thinking step, it's easy to "genially trick ourselves into supposing that we have planned when, in fact, we've only listed some 'good things to do,' like increase sales 5%." Moreover, lists encourage people to be "intellectually lazy" because they're too generic (applicable to any company), leave relationships unspecified, and omit critical assumptions about how the business works.

Shaw sensed he might find a better way buried in the story-intensive nature of 3M's culture, since planning and storytelling share many characteristics. "Planning by narrative is a lot like traditional storytelling," he wrote in the *Harvard Business Review* article. "Like a good storyteller, the strategic planner sets the stage by defining the current situation (industry economics, key success factors, forces that drive change, basic tensions, and relationships—many factors involving complex analyses). Next, the planner introduces the dramatic conflict, such as challenges the company faces and obstacles to success. Finally, the planner's story reaches resolution—how the company can overcome obstacles and win."

The narrative style forces the writer's assumptions to the surface, encourages clear thinking, and brings out the subtlety and complexity of ideas because good storytelling, like good writing, requires a disciplined mind. "Flaws in logic jump right off the page," Shaw noted.

The first time Shaw applied this narrative approach to long-range planning, he found the experience equal parts pain and exhilaration. He started with 30 pages of notes, then wrote, rewrote, and rewrote some more.

All that self-discipline meant Shaw had the storyline down cold before he walked into the conference room, turned off the overhead projector, and said, "I'm going to have fun today." He could hear the assembled managers whispering about impending disaster as they gave each other knowing looks.

However, as Shaw began walking his audience through the planning agenda (the complex science surrounding the business unit of a highly complicated industry, descriptions of the players, the critical issues, and the proposed solution), he soon realized the listeners were making the connections he wanted them to make as he led them from one section of the presentation to the next.

Any good narrative, he wrote, "tells a story of a struggle between opponents in which the good guy triumphs by doing a series of smart things in the right order," just as a solid strategic plan should. Through the narrative, the audience discovers the author's thought processes, so people know far more than they would if given a bulleted list. More than that, "Presenting a plan in narrative creates a richer picture of strategy, not only for the plan's authors, but also for its intended audience."

Just as importantly, Shaw believes, if people can locate themselves in the story, they'll identify with the goal at the end. Like a solid strategic plan, a good story, with a point that becomes clear through the telling, galvanizes both managers and employees to action.

At the end of his presentation, the audience's enthusiastic reaction proved they identified with the plan and bought into its provisions, and their feedback convinced Shaw that narration has the capacity to illuminate the planning process and link the logical left brain with the holistic right—a principle benefit of storytelling, according to Diane Cory and Paula Underwood in an essay in *Learning Organizations*.

"Stories are a habit of mind at 3M," Shaw wrote, "and it's through them—through the way they make us see ourselves and our business operations in complex, multidimensional forms—that we're able to discover opportunities for strategic change."

Like everyone else, Steve Webster liberally sprinkles stories wherever he goes, including a speech for the Tech Forum about the future of 3M™ Multilayer Optical Film. The quarterly internal Forum is a 53-year-old tradition that builds a sense of community, primarily among the company's scientists, although it's open to all. Understanding that a presentation needs to awaken an audience's broader senses to be effective, Webster jumpstarted his talk with the story of the film's development. He drew portraits of each of the key players before articulating how they turned the film into a major growth opportunity for 3M.

In the future, if 3M is to maintain its lead in a number of markets—health care, industrial, consumer and office, electronics, telecommunications, safety, and security, to name a few—leaders must focus on "making the fundamental changes necessary to improve our competitive advantage," says W. James McNerney, Jr., Chairman and CEO.

One fundamental change that will be implemented over the next several years is that, as Webster describes it, "Managers also will identify and reward a different kind of hero—a problem *preventer*, rather than an eleventh-hour problem solver." Both hold the key to 3M's long-term success. Aligned with 3M's Six Sigma initiative, Webster is already communicating problem prevention, using stories about his own failures as examples.

"When I see a program that's headed off in the wrong direction, instead of criticizing the plan, I often tell a pet story to show what *not* to do." His point is to suggest that employees "may want to think hard before they end up having to fix a problem when it's almost too late."

One of his stories goes back to his time as manager of the Data Storage Diskette Lab. "In one program, every molecule of our 2MB (megabit) diskette was new, manufacturing processes were new, and the product had significant features, advantages, and benefits. The 2MB diskette had the largest first-year new-product sales in 3M history and saved our company money, but at the end of the day, it was still a 2MB diskette to users, and 3M didn't create any additional sales."

Webster's team redesigned the 2MB diskette into the 120MB diskette, but a competitor ate 3M's lunch because it hit the market nine months after the 100MB ZIP Disk from IOmega. "In part because of that time difference, 120MB has never been as big as ZIP. In retrospect, we should have killed the 2MB redesign and put everyone on the new-to-the-world product."

If he catches 3Mers thinking inside the box, Webster hauls out another story. "When we showed Multilayer Optical Film, we always showed roses, bows, bags, and other nice decorative applications, because they looked stunning. But the technology's greatest value is in its application to polarized light, or light outside the visible spectrum. In these cases, the film is clear to the eye and really quite boring to look at. When we shared it with customers in the right market, though, they immediately saw the value and made the optical film application a big success."

Cory and Underwood, authors of "Stories for Learning," wrote that narratives are circles with a beginning and ending, but the real value of a learning story is when it expands into a spiral of growth and creativity, like Webster's tales do.

"It's fun when you hear your own anecdotes a year later from people who are unaware they originated with you," Webster laughs.

For more information on the 3M story, go to www.3m.com.

4

K/P Corporation: What's Love Got To Do With It?

Anyone reading K/P Corporation's three core values for the first time is likely to do a double take, particularly on the third one. But there is no mistake. It's right there in black and white in a sophisticated eight-page booklet that eloquently outlines the company's philosophy, history, vision, mission, and objectives. It's that four-letter word spelled l-o-v-e, and it's one of the three corporate values listed on Page One.

Beginning the booklet with Peter Drucker's observation that a business is a human organization whose success depends on the quality of its people, K/P goes on to say that its overriding purpose is to "enable people to do something worth doing so that they can feel they are someone worth being." To fulfill that purpose, the organization seeks to attract and retain people who share the following core values:

- We believe each person in the organization must fully accept responsibility for successfully completing the work he or she is assigned or accepts.
- We believe in the importance of always searching for intellectual honesty, and being honest with ourselves about whether we are true to our own convictions.
- We believe the most important result of a successful career is the love that develops over time among people who work together. When all is said and done, our relationships with each other are our most significant and lasting possessions.

Rich Barbee, President and CEO, says, ""People (myself included) are drawn to this company because they want to improve themselves as a person and improve their quality of life. K/P provides the opportunity to do both. We measure success internally by how people feel about their work at the end of the day. Our customers measure us on our performance to their requirements and how we make them feel about the interactions with our employees. Generally, all involved feel great about the relationships, and the employees and customers stay a part of the K/P family for a long time."

Barbara Webster, Senior Vice President of Sales, says that prospective employees are surprised when they learn that love is one of K/P's fundamental values. They don't usually express their amazement, though, until they've been part of the company for a few months. "Then it's common for them to tell their coworkers that at first they were skeptical, but over time realized that it's true. To anyone who spends time here, it's obvious that we're always striving to show that level of care for one another."

One example, says Marketing Director Barbara Silverman, is that coworkers purposefully help one another succeed instead of competing for top position because they understand that individual achievement is secondary to group success. "Initially the business was structured as a holding company, and each facility was an independent operating unit responsible for its own sales and success. As fluctuations in local economies caused sales downturns in some units, there was some solace in knowing that other facilities' stronger performances would compensate, but true to form, K/P took it one step farther. Putting their own agendas on hold, a team of top sales people and managers from throughout the company converged on an area where sales were down to help 'blitz' that market. They made sales calls, plotted strategy and worked closely with the local division's employees. They had nothing more to gain than the camaraderie of fellow workers and the satisfaction of helping a sister facility out of a jam.

"Eventually, just hours before the salespeople arrived for a company-wide sales meeting in San Diego, the facility presidents decided to give up some of their operational autonomy so the company as a whole could better serve our customers. That was one of the first steps toward becoming the integrated company we are today."

Originally a traditional printing company, K/P was founded in 1929 in Salem, Oregon, as a family-owned business. Now headquartered in San Ramon, California, it's become one of the leading companies in the U.S. that provide a full complement of direct marketing products and services (printing, mailing, fulfillment, research, and evaluation of ROI) integrated through technology. Growing from 15 employees at one shop to more than 600 people at 11 facilities throughout the West, K/P posted modest growth for many years while experiencing a number of identity crises. In an eight-page corporate history that second-generation owner Jim Knapp completed and distributed to employees in June 2000, he chronicles the series of management systems he tried before realizing there's no magic-bullet technique that ensures continuing success. Instead, he discovered a simple truth that became the foundation of the K/P story.

As Knapp tells the story, K/P can trace its beginnings to as early as 1875, when one of the businesses he acquired first opened its doors. The company's official birth is 1929, the year his father became a partner in an existing printing business. Nearly 30 years later, Knapp's father bought out his partner, named the operation Knapp Printing Company, and welcomed his son as General Manager. Brimming with ideas for building a conglomerate, the eager young manager made his first big move in 1968. He bought a Portland printing company, the first of many acquisitions. That move led to a turning point in his life—and in the business.

Working together through the transition, Knapp and the owner of the Portland shop, George Bovik, got to know one another very well. Knapp even lived with Bovik and his wife for a time. One day, when Knapp intimated to the newly-retired 76-year-old that something was missing from his life, but he didn't know what, Bovik shared his story. He said that when he himself was a young man, he gained the insight that there's only one yardstick for measuring whether a life is well-lived. That yardstick is the amount of love remaining among one's coworkers, family and friends over the years.

Bovik's simply-stated observation had a profound effect on Knapp and changed his approach to running the business. Instead of chasing after the latest management trend, he reworked K/P's purpose statement and defined the values system that still serves as the cornerstone of the business. Based on his conviction that people should enact their values in their personal lives as well as their work lives, Knapp believes it's important to hire people who share the company's three core values—accepting responsibility, maintaining intellectual honesty, and loving one another. By doing that, he says, the management team achieves alignment throughout the company, and the culture is continually strengthened in the process.

A natural storyteller, the now-retired Knapp kept in touch with how people were feeling by sharing some of his favorite stories each month when he and a small group of executives visited every plant. He would highlight one of the company's core values and then illustrate how it was being enacted. He also walked around to hear the stories employees were telling one another, and he learned that employees, too, believed the company would continue to succeed as long as they adhered to the values.

Determined to prove that a caring workplace can be profitable, Knapp constantly sought ways to improve the organization. Despite what he terms "wrenching changes" that included the complex process of merging a group of independently-run facilities into one centralized organization, K/P has enjoyed healthy growth, primarily through acquisitions in the early years of his tenure. The company is frequently honored with industry awards for quality work, adding 12 medals and two Honorable Mentions at one event alone. Continuing a longstanding commitment to Total Quality Management practices, K/P proudly announced in Fall 2003 that the Salt Lake City facility was the latest division to earn ISO 9001 certification. Calling the "Six Management Actions" the "Six Human Actions," K/P put its own stamp on TQM practices, asserting that quality is not a program but the way the company chooses to do business.

One of Knapp's most rewarding moves came in recent years. It followed extensive research he conducted to determine the answer to a pressing issue. How can I ensure the success of the company after I'm no longer involved, he had asked himself, and, even more importantly, how can I ensure that the current values remain intact? He considered several possibilities, including going public, merging, selling to a larger company, or creating an employee trust. He discovered that employees didn't care which option he chose "as long as it didn't mess up the culture we had worked so hard to develop for so many years." He finally concluded that the answer to the dilemma was relatively simple. He would sell the company to the employees, a process he initiated in 1997. "The one thing that means the most to me and most others in the company is preserving our purpose and values system," he explained. "No one else has a greater interest in preserving what we've created than the people working here every day." Knapp also believes that employee ownership will encourage and enable everyone who wants to lead to do so, at least some of the time. Defining a leader as anyone who steps forward to bring about positive change in the company, his hope is that most will choose to take on that role.

K/P's commitment to its stated values is evident in many other ways, perhaps the most noticeable being the warm and unusually courteous tone of the employee manual. Rather than enumerating policies and procedures, it describes how K/P treats people and how they should treat one another. Clarifying the values behind the desired behaviors, the guidelines begin with "please" and end with "thank you." For example, the section on safety rules begins by explaining that love is a core value and love means caring about each other's safety. The safety guidelines include directions on pointing out unsafe practices to anyone who is being careless and reporting unsafe conditions to facility managers.

One of the ways the company shows love for people is by treating them gently and respectfully, even when they violate corporate values. Webster tells the story of two Seattle employees who were fired because they were caught smoking pot in the parking lot. The facility president distributed a memo explaining that the two had been let go because "they had made a poor personal decision," a term that's used at that facility to refer to rules violations. "It reminds everyone that we are all responsible for our actions and that we need to be ready to suffer the consequences," she explains.

In another section of the employee manual, everyone is urged to offer positive reinforcement for individual and team accomplishments, to post accolades on special bulletin boards that are displayed in all the facilities, to celebrate successes at meetings, and to share success stories in the company newsletter. "It feels so good to give positive reinforcement," the manual states. "Let's celebrate often! Please join in the fun!"

Webster says all these practices are tied to the company's emphasis on servant leadership, which means, the Senior Sales Vice President says, "All our leaders should always be asking themselves, 'How am I going to help the people reporting to me?' You can't precisely measure the results, but there are good gauges for assessing how everyone is doing. Mainly, you look at how people are treating one another. You also look at retention. It isn't at all unusual for employees to stay at K/P for as many as 30 or 35 years, which is an unusually long time in this era of frequent job changes."

K/P's leaders also are in the habit of asking for employees' input before making decisions. "That tells them they're valued, they can be heard, and they can make a difference," Webster says. "We've attracted salespeople from larger companies because of that. But we realize that we can't be so inwardly focused that we forget about profits. We've proved that it's possible to be caring and profitable at the same time. Those two objectives are not mutually exclusive."

Of course, customer care is highly valued, too, and the company is willing to go the extra mile to maintain strong customer relationships, even incurring extraordinary expenses when necessary. One story the company uses to illustrate this point is about a project that was behind schedule. It was a direct mail piece with a special offer for people attending a trade show, so timing was critical. To get the delivery to the customer in New York on time, Dan Plunkett, now Senior Vice President of Operations who was the Division President at that time, hired a Lear jet. That happened years ago, and that company is still an active and valued customer.

Leaders are responsible for setting the tone, Webster says, and it isn't what they say or do that counts as much as how they make people feel. That's what people remember. That's also what employees enjoy telling stories about, as Webster has learned when she's asked the sales team to share their successes at staff meetings. "It's so much more effective than having me or someone from outside the sales organization telling them what works. Everyone likes to have an opportunity to tell their stories, and allowing people to be heard is another way we show our love for one another."

Perhaps the most extraordinary example of loving leadership is the story of Jean McClellan and Susie Glikbarg. Now working part-time in accounting, McClellan was a supervisor at a California facility when Glikbarg was hired in 1985 and assigned to her team. Born with severe birth defects, Glikbarg struggles with many physical disabilities, including deafness. She communicates verbally and through sign language, but when she was hired, most people couldn't understand her speech and no one at K/P knew sign language. Thinking it would help Glikbarg communicate, McClellan enrolled her right away in a typing class, but that didn't work well. So McClellan decided to learn to sign, and "without a second thought, K/P gave me permission to take two hours off during the day to attend American Sign Language classes a couple of times a week at a local community college." To strengthen her own language skills, Glikbarg began attending the classes with McClellan, and the company allowed both to attend during work hours.

Then, discovering that Glikbarg enjoyed art, McClellan searched for an art program for developmentally-disabled adults in the Oakland area. She found one that allowed people to attend just once a week. K/P readily agreed to allow Susie Glikbarg to work only four days a week so she could attend art classes one day. Showing her appreciation, the fledgling artist included a painting of a K/P truck among her first works, and the company exhibited her work in the lobby of the facility.

Over the years, the two women have developed a strong personal bond as the former supervisor has helped the loyal employee obtain government support, arrange for special medical care, and locate a group home. McClellan has become Glikbarg's interpreter and personal companion, often accompanying her to company functions and other events.

Despite her struggles, McClellan says, "Susie is one of the happiest employees K/P has ever had. She is always smiling and upbeat, an eager worker, and delighted by things most of the rest of us take for granted. She is loved and treasured by everyone at the company."

Orlando Boleda, President of the Washington Division, adds, "We realize that 100% of our employees aren't 100% feeling love for one another 100% of the time. It's a risky thing to tell someone you love them, especially in a business setting, but K/P is an exceptional company, and many people here do just that. We expect everyone to be a good steward of our culture, which leads to a common purpose and, in turn, sustains the culture."

At first glance, the mention of love seems startlingly out of place in a business setting. But it's clear from the K/P story and the experiences of the people who work there that a caring environment can produce an effective, profitable organization. What's love got to do with it? Love has everything to do with business—if you work at K/P Corporation.

For more information on the K/P story, go to www.kpcorp.com.

5

Eastman Kodak: Eight Words Are Enough

Sometimes a company runs the risk of telling a story that's almost *too* good. Once the story is embedded in people's minds, the challenge of keeping it fresh—and relevant—can seem daunting, especially when technology threatens to render the company's signature product obsolete.

Over 100 years ago, the Kodak name was born and its camera was introduced to the market with the company's first advertising slogan: "You press the button, we do the rest."™ Today George Eastman's 1888 slogan is far more than just a marketing promise. It defines Eastman Kodak Company's way of doing business and epitomizes its reputation as the world's original picture-taking company.

"The story is iconic in its power," says Paula K. Dumas, Vice President and Director, Industry Marketing. "If you were to look for one thing employees believe in religiously, it's that the company remain faithful to that ethic, so it's a story that still works for us."

But what's a company founded in 1880 supposed to do when it's so inextricably identified with photos on paper and point-and-shoot cameras, and new technologies are taking over? Dumas and other executives and managers have expended a lot of energy answering that question in recent years. "A whole new industry has emerged, called infoimaging, that recognizes the convergence of imaging science and information technology. Not exclusive to Kodak, infoimaging is an industry category like e-business, and imaging companies, technology companies, and networking companies are all participating."

The competition has been fierce, and according to Kodak's corporate statements, the slump in the U.S. economy has magnified the problem. While market share has remained strong in consumer markets, the travel industry's two-year downturn meant there were fewer vacationers taking pictures. At the same time, consumer digital cameras surged in popularity, and in response to a decline in its historic film business, Kodak announced in September 2003 that the company would focus on its growing digital businesses. It proved to be a good move. During a period of significant workforce cuts and dips in earnings, Kodak consumer digital cameras were the top-selling brand during the 2003 holiday season.

Kodak's annual sales had dropped from more than $14 billion in 1999 to under $13 billion in 2002, but recovered to $13.3 billion at the end of 2003. Net earnings for the year totaled $265 million, or 92 cents a share, compared with $770 million, or $2.64 per share, in 2002.

Stock prices plummeted from $83.88 in July 1998 to $22.15 by September 2003, the lowest price in nearly 20 years. But by early 2004 shares had risen to above $28 a share.

To stem the downward trend and re-invest in new imaging opportunities, Kodak slashed its dividend in September 2003 by more than 2/3—its first cut ever—and redirected the funds to establishing its pre-eminent position in the infoimaging industry.

"This is probably the biggest turning point in our recent history," Chairman and CEO Daniel A. Carp told investors in New York. "When you fuse traditional imaging, digital imaging, and next-generation information technologies, infoimaging represents the moment images actually become information," Dumas explains.

Carp says most people think of pictures only as a great way to save personal memories. "Increasingly, technology makes it possible for pictures to also significantly impact the way businesses serve their customers and make money. Through infoimaging, we see moving and still images as a key driver of value, growth, and understanding. Infoimaging has the potential to profoundly change how people and businesses communicate and work together, to create tools that can bring world-class medical treatment to every corner of the globe, to make virtual reality less virtual and more real, and to bring families closer together."

As explained on the company's story-rich Web site, six billion inhabitants of this planet speak more than 3,000 languages, but only one is shared by all of us: pictures. Images are information. Without them, the Worldwide Web would have remained an academic curiosity, e-commerce wouldn't exist, and a huge industry would never have been born.

Infoimaging is at work when people share digital images of landscape and development property via cell phones, transmitting them to architects and developers at off-site locations. No longer a novelty for consumers, picture-enabled cell phones have created new market opportunities for both imaging companies and wireless providers. According to projections by market research firms such as IDC, more than a billion camera-enabled mobile phones will be in use by the end of 2006.

Responding to this new phone technology, Kodak announced plans in November, 2003, to provide mobile imaging services that help people store, share, organize and print their digital images. Agreements with Cingular Wireless and Nokia enable Kodak Mobile Service to provide camera phone users anytime, anywhere access to all of their digital photos and phone-captured video. And in early 2004, Kodak announced it would enable its Kodak Picture Maker digital printing kiosks in retail locations to receive, enhance, and print mobile phone images sent wirelessly from handset to kiosk.

Infoimaging is priceless when more than 28,000 radiologists and related professionals on opposite sides of the globe share X-rays and health data for patient diagnosis. To share these detailed images, many health care professionals rely on private networks and picture-archiving communications systems (PACS) designed and installed by Kodak Health Imaging and its technology partners. The technology also is priceless when new parents in San Francisco share a picture of their baby over the Internet, including information on length, weight, and health, with friends and relatives in Boston and New York. They even have a choice of tools—a selection of wired or wireless devices, perhaps coupled with the Kodak-AOL partnership called "You've Got Pictures". sm

An industry already worth approximately $400 billion, infoimaging quickly grew to 4.5 times the size of the photography business and is expected to far outstrip the growth of traditional photography. Steven Minton, director of the worldwide IT market research group at tech tracker IDC in Framingham, Massachusetts, estimated 2004 growth of 7% to 8% for the entire business technology market in the U.S., and IDC predicted business IT spending globally would grow 5%, from $874 billion to $915 billion.

Kodak has the distinction among its competitors of being a major player in all three categories of infoimaging:

- The $185 billion devices market (products such as computers, digital cameras, and scanners that capture and deliver images coupled with information)

- The $52 billion infrastructure market (hardware and software to transport and store information and images, such as optical networks, routers, switches, imaging software, and retail photofinishing networks, both online and traditional)
- The $148 services and media industry (photo printing, storing and sharing; document preservation; and photo media, such as film, output paper, and ink)

With so much at stake, Chief Marketing Officer Carl Gustin spurred development of a communication platform to explain an industry not exclusively about Kodak, but about every business that marries information and imaging technologies for both internal and external audiences. Everyone at Kodak—35,500 employees in the U.S. and 64,000 worldwide at the end of 2003—is encouraged to share the infoimaging message to expand the notion of what Kodak's business is all about.

Dumas says, "Several years ago, we began our transition from a picture-taking company to an infoimaging company ready to take advantage of the new digital economy." Many audiences still viewed the company through the film and photo-service lens, despite the fact that Kodak's work led the infoimaging field, but "among the digital innovations pioneered by Kodak were the first commercialized digital camera, organic light-emitting display technology, and the first PDA-based digital camera. Our heritage is at least as much digital as its is analog."

According to the corporate Web site, Kodak inventors were issued 19,576 U.S. patents in the 20th century, with 23% issued between 1995 and 1999. By 2003, 190 Kodak inventors had earned at least 20 U.S. patents, and three had been awarded more than 100. Syamal K. Ghosh leads the group with 136.

Other companies might have come up with a proprietary new slogan to introduce a new industry. Not Kodak. While the company introduced "infoimaging" to the business lexicon, it didn't copyright it. Instead, Kodak made infoimaging broadly available for other businesses, analysts, and media to embrace and cover. Reflecting the importance of the new industry, *Forbes* has devoted a portion of its own Web site to coverage of a variety of infoimaging companies.

At the same time that Kodak pursues new opportunities, the company's annual report clearly reaffirms George Eastman's commitment to ease-of-use in new products. A new family of consumer digital cameras—the Kodak EasyShare system—included the 2001 introduction of a docking station that recharges the camera and automatically loads photos onto the user's computer screen. "You press the button, we do the rest" also graced the cover of Kodak's 2000 annual report.

EasyShare fulfills the promise created by Eastman, but in the digital realm. "With its one-button simplicity, the EasyShare system helps reinforce the value of pictures as a storytelling medium," Dumas says. "Most EasyShare digital cameras let users enter email addresses of friends and family, and a red button on the camera lets them 'tag' photos for emailing to those addresses. When they dock the camera, the pictures are downloaded and emailed."

"You press the button, we do the rest." This eight-word "story" is the core of Kodak's identity, as a well-told, values-based corporate story should be. "We still like our story," Dumas says, "but we want people to know there's more. The real challenge rests with our ability to make that ease-of-use story relevant in a world where pressing a button is no longer a novelty. We need to expand on that story that's already implanted in people's minds."

The "more" Dumas refers to can be found in many of Kodak's communications tools. Employees received toolkits to help explain and understand the infoimaging umbrella, and where their products and services fit into the continuum of infoimaging devices, infrastructure, and services and media. Externally—in addition to the *Forbes* Web site—infoimaging is part of the lexicon used by industry analysts.

Stories on the company's Web site also underscore the infoimaging industry's link to Kodak's future. One of only a few companies involved in all three segments of the infoimaging industry, Kodak "touches" three out of four images on the Internet, and the company expects to participate in new segments of the market where the technology applies. Kodak Mobile Imaging, which didn't exist when the infoimaging concept emerged in 2000, "is an example of the company's agility in applying its digital prowess to new opportunities," Dumas said.

He calls the infoimaging storytelling effort a "powerful example of how the way you talk about yourself influences what you can do. The growth of the infoimaging market is exhilarating to Kodak people, who are eager to see market growth in new areas where Kodak has a technological advantage." The story of this emerging industry has changed the way the company views itself, to the point where its communications often tie new technologies and innovations to the infoimaging industry.

Recognizing Kodak's leadership in other areas, *Business Ethics* magazine named the company one of the "100 Best Corporate Citizens" for 2003, noting its top-tier strengths in its diversity programs, community/education support, employee relations, and pollution-prevention programs. The company has also been named among the "Top 30 Companies for Executive

Women" by the National Association for Female Executives (NAFE).

Over the past 20 years, many companies have showcased photos of people at work in their annual reports. The obvious reason: Without people, there *is* no company. Naturally Kodak does this too, but with an additional twist. In the 2001 Kodak report, photo stories of employees' on-the-job contributions were featured along with a glimpse of the person outside the workplace. It was an approach true to another of the company's advertising themes: "Share moments. Share life."

The story on José Mir, Senior Research Associate, says he creates poetry in Spanish, historical novelas in English, and collects multicultural art. On the job, he explores "immersive imaging," an innovation that promises to place viewers inside the image they're viewing.

Storytelling also helps Kodak's senior managers explain their approach to transforming their icon-based business. Antonio Perez, named Kodak's President and Chief Operating Officer in 2003, shared stories of his family upbringing and the family's passion for dinner-table debate in the January 2004 *DiversityInc.* magazine. Debate, he says, is essential in plotting a business strategy. "The beautiful thing about debate is not that you win the debate, it's that you participate in it. That's what engages you. You are contributing to build the final solution."

As the company raises its profile, other managers' successes and achievements have become public examples of Kodak's focus on its people as success stories. Karen Smith-Pilkington, Senior Vice Chairman of Kodak's Greater Asia Region, and Antoinette McCorvey, Vice President of Corporate Financial Planning and Analysis, both were profiled in *Profiles in Diversity Journal,* where they described the experiences that helped shape their careers.

At a diversity workshop on a local college campus, CEO Carp shared a personal story with attendees, explaining that the way his parents conducted their business had a lasting effect on his view of customer service. His parents, who were shop owners, showed equal respect for all their customers, even those who couldn't afford to buy much. Feedback from the students indicated that Carp's 2-3-minute story had an astonishing impact, touching them more deeply than any story they heard, or any picture they saw, the entire day.

Carp's story was a living example of "Share Moments. Share Life." It expressed a way of life espoused and lived by other company executives as well, just as Eastman himself expressed his ethic so simply in 1888. As explained on the company's Web site 115 years later, "What George Eastman began remains a goal of Eastman Kodak Company today: to provide convenience and quality to our customers so more and more people can experience the special wonders of photography and capture and relive their more cherished moments."

Even as the company embarks on new opportunities in a world of rapidly changing picture-taking choices, Kodak's leaders pledge not to lose sight of the simple, elegant promise of "You press the button, we do the rest." The user-friendliness implied by George Eastman's story is every bit as fresh, and just as relevant, today as when Eastman created it.

"We've used 'Take Pictures. Further.' We've used 'Share Moments, Share Life.' And we will likely find occasions to use other messages to tell the Kodak story in the future," Dumas adds. "But we have found, time and again, that user-friendliness and ease-of-use are what consumers want most. And Eastman's promise says that in a unique way."

Sometimes a founder's original "story," even one as short as eight words, rises to the challenge.

For more information on the Kodak story, go to www.kodak.com.

6

Costco Wholesale: A Genuine Fish Story

Repeating favorite stories about everyday practices is one of the ways Costco Wholesale managers continually remind employees of the company's founding values. President and CEO Jim Sinegal says one of his favorite stories is about Calvin Klein jeans, and it's one he tells often to illustrate Costco's commitment to ensuring good value for customers.

"We were selling Calvin Klein jeans for $29.99, and we were selling every pair we could get our hands on. One competitor matched our price, but they had only four or five pairs in each store, and we had 500 or 600 pairs on the shelf. We all of a sudden got our hands on several million pairs of Calvin Klein jeans, and we bought them at a very good price. It meant that, within the constraints of our markup, which is limited to 14% on any item, we had to sell them for $22.99. That was $7 lower than we had been selling every single pair for.

"Of course, we concluded that we could have sold all of them (about four million pairs) for that higher price almost as quickly as we sold them at $22.99, but there was no question that we would mark them at $22.99 because that's our philosophy.

"I use that as an example because it would be so tempting for a buyer to go with the higher price for a very quick $28 million in additional profits, and ours didn't. That's an example of how we keep faith with our customers."

"When we do things like that on a consistent basis, there's never any question in anybody's mind—our buyers, our warehouse managers, the people who work on the sales floor—and never any question in the minds of our customers because we're always honest with them."

The founders of Costco Wholesale were clear about their values when they launched the wholesale warehouse company in 1983, and they haven't wavered one iota since. They remain firmly committed to the clearly articulated principles that form the company's code of ethics:

- Obey the law.
- Take care of members.
- Take care of employees.
- Respect suppliers.
- Take care of shareholders.

Sitting in the Issaquah, Washington, corporate headquarters, Sinegal explained that these principles are simply stated, and easy to understand and follow. "All our energy goes toward figuring out how we can improve products and bring goods to market at a lower price. We've made this our mantra because that's what we stand for."

In addition to telling stories about examples of desired behavior, Costco ensures that everyone understands those principles through employee training and by consistently reinforcing the company's code of ethics. Sinegal's statement on the corporate Web site is one example: "Costco is able to offer lower prices and better values by eliminating virtually all the frills and costs historically associated with conventional wholesalers and retailers, including salespeople, fancy buildings, delivery, billing, and accounts receivable. We run a tight operation with extremely low overhead, which enables us to pass on dramatic savings to our members."

In developing the company's strategic plan, Costco's founders recognized that "it's kind of a crazy business—cement floors, open ceilings, a big warehouse, forklifts running around, and all this merchandise stacked to the ceiling. With great prices always on the merchandise, we figured people would wonder, 'What's the catch?'" Sinegal says.

"So we formulated our business on the basis of eliminating all the potential objections. We never, ever sell distressed merchandise, we pay our employees more than any other retailer in the city, and we decided we wouldn't advertise or put up signs in the warehouses claiming lots of superlatives. We also decided to guarantee every single product unconditionally.... If someone buys a TV from us and drops it from a third floor window, then brings it back to us saying they're unhappy with it, we'll give them their money back."

He smiles as he launches into another legendary tale. "But probably no story tells what we do relative to the products and value better than the salmon story." Jumping up to get a copy of a management presentation illustrating the story, Sinegal begins thumbing through the pages as he excitedly launches into the retelling.

"In 1996 we were selling between $150,000 and $200,000 worth of salmon filets company wide every week at $5.99 a pound. Then our buyers were able to get an improved product, with belly fat, back fins, and collarbones removed, at a better price. As a result, we reduced our retail price to $5.29. So they improved the product *and* lowered the price!"

The buyers weren't finished with the improvements, though. "Next our buyers negotiated for a product with the pin bone out and all of the skin removed, and it was at an even better price, which enabled us to lower our price to $4.99 a pound. Then, because we had continued to grow and had increased our sales volume, we were able to buy direct from

Canadian and Chilean farms, which resulted in an even lower price of $4.79.

"Over a five-year period, a significantly enhanced product was lowered from $5.99 a pound to $4.79." And still the story kept getting better. "The final improvement was that the belly was removed, and customers get the top filet, and the price further reduced to $3.99 a pound."

Customers have shown their appreciation for this genuine fish story. Salmon sales over the same five-year period increased more than ten-fold, from $150,000-$200,000 per week to almost $2 million per week.

Sinegal says, "We've used that story so much as a teaching tool that I've had other buyers in the company, such as a clothing buyer in Canada, come up to me and say, 'Hey, I've got a salmon story to tell you.' That story explains the essence of what we do." And it's become part of Costco lore.

The Costco philosophy is also exhibited in the way the company treats employees. Sinegal's partner and cofounder, Chairman Jeff Brotman, speaks for both when he says, "If you hire good people, give them good jobs, and pay them good wages, good things will happen."

Employees echo this view. Working with a representative group of 25 warehouse managers, an external consultant was surprised to learn that most had been with the company at least 10 years, a relatively long term of employment in an age of frequent job and career changes. Invariably, when each manager was asked, "Why have you stayed with Costco so long?" the answer was, "Because the company is good to its employees."

As Alex Polo, manager of a Costco warehouse in Bayamón, Puerto Rico, explained in the employee magazine, *Costco Today*, "A lot of good people took an interest in me, recognized my abilities, and encouraged me to go further....

This company means everything to me. Many of my values and the way I handle myself ethically are a mirror image of this company.... I'm just happy to be here."

One unusual policy demonstrates just how well Costco treats its people. After employees have been with the company for two years, they can't be dismissed without the approval of a senior executive.

Sinegal explains, "If we lose an employee, it's a failing on our part as well as theirs. One of the few ways employees can get into serious trouble is by doing something dishonest. We insist that our people understand that they are never to do anything dishonest. We don't want them to lie to our customers, we don't want them to lie to our suppliers, and we certainly don't want them to deceive the communities we live and work in."

Named one of *Business Week's* "Best Managers of 2002," Sinegal is a down-to-earth leader who personally participates in every new warehouse opening. He also enjoys taking part in management training classes because he wants everyone to understand the Costco approach to decision making.

"Respect for the law, our customers, our fellow employees, and our suppliers is the hallmark of our business. We think if you do that, you'll come out OK, and you'll do what you're supposed to do, which is to reward your shareholders. That's ultimately the responsibility of any public company. We think it's possible to do that without those first four steps in the short term, but we don't think it's possible in the long term. You're going to trip yourself up in the long term."

When asked how he knows the Costco philosophy is working, Sinegal responds with a smile, "How do you know when anything's working? Business may be down because the economy is not so hot, or there was bad weather. Retailers never run out of excuses. We may run out of eggs, we may run out of ground beef, but we never run out of excuses. [The only way to know if our approach is working is] to measure the success of the business as well as public opinion."

By any measure, Costco's approach has worked. Keeping overhead extremely low and passing the savings on to customers has enabled Costco to capture 50% of the wholesale club market. After a merger with Price Club in 1995, Costco began tracing its history to the start of Price Club in 1976. At the end of 2003, nearly 28 years later, the company had grown to 103,000 employees and 430 warehouses across 36 U.S. states and Puerto Rico, Canada, Mexico, the U.K., Korea, Taiwan, and Japan. And the company was keeping a steady pace, adding 10 stores per month.

Nearly 20 million members generated record sales for the company of $41.69 billion in FY2003, a 10% increase over the previous year, and same-store sales increased 4% for the year. With a membership renewal rate of 86%, Costco's track record affirms the proposition that customers will recognize value and reward it with loyal patronage. Even in 2003's tight economy, the company managed a 3% increase in profits.

Himself a regular customer at Costco's hot dog window, the down-to-earth Sinegal backs up his claims of customer satisfaction with results of the American Customer Satisfaction Index (ACSI). The study is conducted by the University of Michigan Business School's National Quality Research Center in partnership with the American Society for Quality (ASQ) and CFI Group, an international consulting firm. Costco has ranked #1 among specialty retailers four of the five years the company has been included in the survey, coming in a close second the year it dropped from the lead. Costco was back on top for the fourth quarter of 2003, regaining a significant edge over competitors with its highest score ever.

Professor Claes Fornell, director of the National Quality Research Center and Chairman of CFI Group, says that a key to Costco's high level of customer satisfaction "appears to be a strong commitment to its workers. Wages and benefits are among the highest in the industry. Another factor is that it offers both high-end and private label discount products."

Sinegal uses the company's growth as a measure of its success in imparting its values even without advertising or a PR staff. "Our values are so simple, we don't have to worry about all that. Our view is that it's always better if somebody else says something good about you than if you say it yourself; that has a lot more credibility.

"If you asked 100 people what they think when they hear the Costco name," Sinegal speculates, "the typical response would be one of the following: big stuff or bulk, great prices, quality, value, and a fantastic hot dog and Coke for $1.50!"

For more information on the Costco story, go to www.costco.com.

7

Mary Kay: Putting Women In The Driver's Seat

On the way to building a multibillion-dollar global cosmetics empire, Mary Kay Ash used the power of storytelling more effectively, and imprinted her personality on a business more indelibly, than perhaps any business leader in recent memory.

When she died in November 2001 at 83 after a five-year illness, Mary Kay (as she is fondly referred to, like Lucy, Oprah, and other first-name icons) left behind a grieving "family" of more than 1.1 million independent sales force members and 3,600 employees, as well as a legacy of caring unsurpassed in today's business world. Mary Kay's Dallas-based cosmetics empire was launched in 1963 with $5,000; a dream of enriching women's lives; and advice from her son, current Chairman and CEO Richard R. Rogers. It's now one of the largest direct sellers of skin-care products based in the United States. The company offers more than 200 products in more than 30 international markets, sold more than $1.8 billion wholesale in 2003, does a better job of creating leaders than almost any other company in the world, and uses stories to reinforce the legacy.

Using stories as a way to motivate others evolved naturally for Ash. At first she fired up her sales force by sharing details of her own early life as a widowed working mother. For four decades, her story has continued to inspire recruits to embrace her dream of personal and financial success and make it their own. Her vision was simple:

Faith first. Family second. Financial success last.

As a business owner, she applied simple principles that resonated with women, such as:

- Find a need and fill it.
- Give women careers, not just products to sell.
- Teach (and lead) by example.
- Encourage other women to do the same.
- Build self-esteem along the way.

"Each time I hear one woman realize how great she is, that makes my day," Ash repeated like a mantra. She also seemed to know intuitively that companies whose leaders look beyond short-term uncertainties and focus on long-term goals fare best in both good times and bad. Her approach was to create a community of women, each with a Mary Kay heart: "Equal parts big business and big sister," noted Laura Klepacki in the New York-based fashion/beauty trade publication *Women's Wear Daily (WWD)*. This approach remains at the heart of the company's mission 40 years later.

In the early days, spreading the word was easy. The independent sales force gathered at Ash's office or house, where she served home-baked cookies. As profits flowed in and the sales force grew, the trappings of her success included larger headquarters and a custom-built pink mansion, complete with a pink, heart-shaped tub in her bathroom. One day, as Ash entertained new independent sales directors at a tea in her home, some of the top saleswomen decided to have their pictures taken in the tub for good luck. What started as a lark evolved into tradition. Even today, new independent sales directors want a photo in that bathtub, and their wishes are accommodated. A pink, heart-shaped bathtub also occupies a prominent place in the office of Tom Whatley, President of Global Sales and Marketing.

What pops into most people's minds when they hear "Mary Kay" is a custom-painted pink Cadillac. Today, some 2000 of Mary Kay Inc.'s top independent beauty consultants drive these trophies-on-wheels, and the color is now a stylish pearlized pink that always draws admiring glances. Another change is that the choice of cars has expanded to include models from BMW, Mercedes, Toyota, and Ford.

Not as well known as the car award is the company's lasting commitment to Ash's lifelong goal: enriching women's lives. Her vision has been transformed into an organization so infused by caring that its corporate leaders quote the founder with sincerity: "P&L stands for people and love, not profit and loss." (After the company went public in 1976, Ash was dismayed with the shift in focus to shareholders and the bottom line, and her family regained ownership in a 1985 leveraged buyout. Mary Kay Inc. remains privately held.)

The genuine warmth and caring of Ash's original dream company are felt by the nearly one million "family members," comprised of independent beauty consultants around the world and employees at corporate headquarters and field locations. The independent sales force serves as the "front line," selling skin-care products to their friends and acquaintances while recruiting other women to expand the sales circle. Team leaders help their recruits stretch beyond the limits some place on themselves. There is an emphasis on team building, and no matter where a recruit relocates in the nation, her attachment to her recruiter remains intact, even though she might be "adopted" by sales force members in her new area. As Ash was fond of saying, "You dance with who brung ya." This concept—unique in the business world—builds life-time relationships, consummate loyalty, and long-term rewards. It also allows career flexibility and feeds a thriving no-territories sales organization.

Mary Kay lore could, and does, fill a volume or two. Over 30 years, Ash wrote three books, all best sellers. Her autobiography, *Mary Kay: You Can Have It All: Lifetime Wisdom from America's Foremost Woman Entrepreneur,* made the U.S. best-seller list within days of its 1995 release date. It eventually sold more than a million copies and has been printed in several languages. Harvard Business School, the Kellogg School of Management, and other universities still cite the founder's philosophy in their case studies, a philosophy outlined in *Mary Kay on People Management* (1984). Another best-seller was published by McGraw-Hill Trade after her death. Written by Jim Underwood, it's a business book titled *More Than A Pink Cadillac: Mary Kay, Inc.'s 9 Leadership Keys to Success.*

Paychecks of the Heart: 113 Inspiring Stories About Living the Principles of Mary Kay Ash (printed in both English and Mandarin Chinese and offered solely to Mary Kay beauty consultants and staff) was the first hardcover book about her that Ash didn't write. It was published in 2000, and several titles exploring her ideas have followed, ranging from money management to cooking.

Personal vignettes in *Paychecks of the Heart* celebrate the company's first generation of leaders and help preserve the Mary Kay tradition of caring. One such "paycheck" involved giving a woman her dignity back. Hazel's dwarfism kept defeating her attempts to get a meaningful job, even though she'd earned a college degree, until she discovered Mary Kay. Now the only help she needs is a box to stand on when she leads beauty classes. The company is a place, Hazel says, where "everyone starts out the same, no matter their stature. Thanks to Mary Kay, when I look in the mirror, I'm just as big as anyone else."

Over the years, Ash's own personal story receded into the background, replaced by the stories of her sales force leaders. There is nothing more inspiring than the rags-to-riches sagas of successful independent beauty consultants, nothing more powerful than the stories of professional women who've come to their new career to find balance in their lives. Ash liked to call them her "daughters," a label invested with all the family feeling such a designation implies. And Ash's recognition of their stories continues to be a powerfully motivating force. Yvonne Pendleton, Director of Corporate Heritage, explains that Mary Kay sells lipstick but, "as our founder always noted, 'this is much more than a cosmetics company.' It's more like a dream factory where women believe in a common purpose and have fun. Every story underscores the lessons that Mary Kay Ash has taught the world."

The result? Big dividends, not only through financial success and a strong bottom line (2002 was the company's fourth consecutive year of record results), but through the enhanced lives of Mary Kay consultants, the people in communities they serve, and their own families. The company founder always insisted that consultants bring their families with them on the journey to economic liberation rather than abandon them, as was often the case in the male-dominated corporations where she had worked before.

Along the way, Ash was honored with the Horatio Alger Distinguished American Citizen Award, and in 1999, Lifetime TV network viewers named her the most influential businesswoman of the 20th century. *Fortune* included Mary Kay Inc. in a number of its trademark lists. Among the highlights: the "100 Best Companies to Work For" three times, including the first list in 1984; the first edition in 1993 of the "10 Best

Companies for Women," and the "Most Admired Corporations in America" in 1995. Another coup: Ash was the only woman featured in *Forbes® Greatest Business Stories of All Time*, published in 1996.

When a debillitating stroke in 1996 forced Ash to abandon day-to-day responsibilities at the empire she had built with love, members of the Mary Kay Inc. family mourned her absence as a personal loss. Their uncertainty about a future without their beloved leader affected product sales and consultant recruitment, which in turn caused the company to realize anew the power of its 30-year culture.

"When Mary Kay was no longer active," recalls Pendleton, "we realized that we had to find ways to become her voice, to find ways to keep her values at the forefront, and to work to maintain the warm, friendly, caring environment of our company. We knew it would now be up to everyone in the organization to fuel the passion."

One of the motivational tools executives used to enrich the independent beauty consultants' passion for excellence was one that the founder had used so effectively: storytelling. "Luckily, we knew from previous experience that, when we failed to sustain our culture through storytelling, it showed up on the bottom line and in the attitudes of our independent sales force," Pendleton explains.

Pat Danforth, a home economist, said she was lured by the "suit, scoop, and loot" of a Mary Kay business, and she's gratified that her business could thrive despite 12 moves in 15 years. Barbara DeLorimiere, former bank teller and secretary, believes she finally earns what *she* is worth, not what the *job* is worth. Lovie Quinn helped her first recruit clean house and baby-sat for the second one because she knew this career was about helping others and touching lives, not just making money. Diane Underwood loves how well the career meshes with motherhood. Sally Rattray, an active military wife, wanted to supplement the decreased income after her husband's retirement, but never dreamed she'd earn so much she could buy him an airplane. These are just some of the stories told in *Room At the Top*, a collection of stories about independent national sales directors that's available to the company's sales force via their intranet.

These stories and others like them are intended to convince readers that "these women are just like me" so they too will be motivated to reach for similar heights. Other pages on the corporate Web site feature tributes to the company's founder, such as one from legendary motivational speaker Zig Ziglar: "Mary Kay spread the good word about life, love and hope so badly needed in America today."

"Every story underlines what makes Mary Kay unique," says Pendleton. "From the immigrant who sewed on buttons when she first came to America, to the bank officer who needed more time to be home with her children."

Progressively, the company began using all its creative resources—from videos, CDs, and magazines to recruiting brochures and the Web site—to enhance its culture. In sharing their stories, the independent national sales directors find common ground to which many other women can relate. That still happens today, as their stories continue to be told.

Yvonne Pendleton has been communicating the company's mission of enriching women's lives for more than 10 years. Bulging archives of success stories provide a rich treasure trove that continues to motivate women in the new century, and the collection of stories led the company to produce *Enriching Lives* videos in 2001 and another video series in 2003.

There are also inspirational accounts in a book that Pendleton edited, *From Our Hearts: 13 Stories of Compassion, Perseverance and Hope.* It tells how independent beauty consultants and staff members' strength gives hope to others in difficult times. The book weaves the "golden thread of compassion that runs deep in the heart of the company, emanating from...Mary Kay Ash," Pendleton wrote in the introduction. Each narrative reflects the philosophy of the Mary Kay Go-Give™ Award that recognizes women for selfless acts of kindness—an honor even more prestigious than the coveted pink Cadillac.

Debbie Bower discovered the depth of that kindness when her teenage daughter was killed in a car accident. During her darkest days, Bower's independent national sales director cried with her every day long-distance by phone and provided the spiritual strength instrumental in giving the grieving mother the will to go on.

Robyn Cartmill, today the proud driver of her own pink Cadillac, recounts how her yesterdays included sleeping in cars, fighting a heroin addiction, and being incarcerated in federal prison. She turned her life around and eventually got a college degree, and her Mary Kay recruiter saw Cartmill's potential rather than her past. Cartmill shares her painful history in the book to inspire others to overcome overwhelming obstacles.

Melanoma-survivor Susan Hibbs' experience with cancer prompted one of her customers to consult a dermatologist about a suspicious mole she'd discovered on her own body. Because Hibbs had shared her story and encouraged her customer to seek a doctor's opinion, she likely saved that woman's life.

Another beneficiary of the Go-Give spirit, Judy Pennington credits her Mary Kay extended family and their countless acts of compassion with making the pain bearable when her 54-year-old father died suddenly of a heart attack, followed by the suicide 10 days later of her 56-year-old mother.

When the Mary Kay Ash Charitable Foundation (MKACF) expanded the causes it supports by adding domestic violence, the company found there were members of its own sales force who were or had been victims of domestic violence. One of those stories was relayed in a poignant *Enriching Lives* video, bringing close to home how widespread this problem is in our society.

Mary Kay's leadership team obviously includes some consummate storytellers, but what they do best is listen. An entire department does nothing but answer letters from the independent sales force. "We want to know how they are feeling and hear their stories. This is a tradition established by Mary Kay Ash. You learn so much...what resonates in the marketplace and what doesn't," Pendleton explains. The listening is also structured into advisory boards from the top ranks of the independent sales force, who are consulted on many sales and marketing initiatives by the leaders in those groups.

"In the 1960s and 1970s, women couldn't wait to get out of the house and start climbing the corporate ladder. Then came burnout, and an 180° turnaround. In the '90s, women wanted to be at home and focus on their children while still building a rewarding business. Because we listen, we're hopefully better able to keep attuned to what motivates women and what they want from a cosmetics company as well as a career."

Staffers also search for stories by asking the sales force to answer (via e-mail) such questions as, *What's special about me and my story?* or, *How has your Mary Kay business enriched your life?* Their responses give the company a never-ending supply of heartwarming tales for motivational publications, meetings, e-mails, videos, and speeches. The stories can be as lighthearted as they are serious.

Mary Kay's monthly magazine, *Applause*®, had overwhelming response when they sent out a call for photos of vanity license plates on pink Cadillacs featuring Mary Kay-isms. One independent sales force member sent in a photo of the pink tractor she purchased for her husband.

"In the field, we learn as much as teach," Pendleton continues. "Mary Kay used to say that 'for many women, the last time they heard cheers was at their high school graduation.' We love the idea that this career provides so many women another chance to feel special, to reach for their dreams."

The stories flow continously. One edition of *Applause* showcased a North Carolina woman whose Mary Kay business profits helped her start a school for other learning-challenged children like her daughter. Another consultant found that her Utah town lacked a women's shelter and helped get one started. Yet another talked about her fight against cancer. These women are among hundreds of thousands inspired by Mary Kay Ash's vision and by the Mary Kay Ash Charitable Foundation.

The Go-Give spirit means service above and beyond the call, and throngs of customers write commendation letters. One told how an independent beauty consultant delivered product to her at the airport so she didn't have to take a business trip without her favorite lipstick. A second customer wrote that, after an Oklahoma City tornado, she hadn't washed her face in three days as she struggled to find order amid the chaos. When her Mary Kay consultant brought a basket of products to what used to be her front door, the customer broke into tears at the kindness. The 2001 terrorist attacks directly affected several members of the Mary Kay family, and the company and independent sales force rallied around them. Not only did the "family" reach out to comfort them, they also contributed to a fund that directly benefited affected family members.

Special stories of heroism take center stage at "Seminar," a series of meetings the company uses to educate, unify, and inspire its sales force. Sometimes the stories, such as the ones that follow, are planned for sharing, and sometimes they just happen.

An independent sales director weakened by chemotherapy could no longer direct motivational meetings for her family of beauty consultants. She couldn't even care for her own customers. Fellow Mary Kay consultants stepped in for six months, kept her business running, ran errands like taking clothes to the dry cleaners, and even walked her dog. When she finally felt better, the consultant took back the reins. In the meantime, her commission checks never stopped. Most important, her Mary Kay business remained intact.

Another independent beauty consultant and her three children traveled cross-country to escape domestic violence. When the consultant's independent sales director back home heard the woman and her family were living in a shelter, she contacted another member of the Mary Kay family living nearby. Could she help? Indeed she could. Since she'd been a victim of physical abuse herself, her strength and support aided the victim in finally breaking the cycle of violence.

During the company's 2002 Seminar in Dallas, there were drawings for a total makeover for the formal Awards Night. The makeovers came complete with a shopping spree, hair stylings, makeup applications, and a limousine to the event. When the woman who won the first drawing was called onstage, a hushed audience learned that she had begun her Mary Kay business after her husband was diagnosed with Lou Gehrig's disease. They had two small children and she needed to help support the family with work she could do at home. There wasn't a dry eye in the house as the woman recounted how "God must have known how much I needed this."

Because Mary Kay executives realize that leadership excellence comes to life when stories are shared, they recognize that the impact of these inspirational stories are both immediate and long lasting. They also believe the effects can be measured.

Since 1999, the company has enjoyed four years of record results. By August 2002, there were more than 900,000 independent beauty consultants worldwide, and during Seminar 2002, 28 women in the U.S. were added to the esteemed ranks of independent national sales directors, the largest class in company history. (During Mary Kay Inc.'s first 36 years, just 150 women earned the right to join the elite group of top earners.)

"We're in the people business, so we focus on the story, but it's not all about the past. It's as much about today and tomorrow as it is about yesterday," Pendleton says. "We also focus on possibilities and breaking belief barriers."

Recognizing that daughters of today's independent sales force form a potent core of Mary Kay Inc.'s future, the company continually introduces new formulations and products to its core lines. In 2001, the Velocity™ product line was introduced, the result of 12 months of research focused on developing products that would appeal to women ages 14 to 24. The initiative demonstrates that the company researches consumer preferences as vigorously as it does stories.

Pendleton says, "In the cosmetics industry, products and packaging have to change, but at Mary Kay Inc., what doesn't change is the people, and the needs of women don't change, and our philosophy doesn't change. Mary Kay Inc. understands that women everywhere in the world want the same thing; they want to feel good about themselves. They want a better life for their families, and they want to be able to help others."

Tom Whatley echoes these sentiments. "We know we are making a difference in women's lives. Even though we've become a big business, we will never lose sight of the fact that Mary Kay Inc. is about helping people. Our mission centers on the spirit of caring, living the positive values Mary Kay built the company on so many years ago, passing her values to new generations. That will never change."

What will change are the lives of everyone associated with Mary Kay, Inc. A powerful businesswoman with a caring heart, Mary Kay Ash built a multibillion-dollar international business by believing in and encouraging others. It's an inspiring legend that will be told even more than the stories of those who followed her lead, the stories she most loved to tell.

For more information on the Mary Kay story, go to www.marykay.com.

8

Fox's Gem Shop: More Than A Little Foxy

Long-time travelers on Alaska Airlines likely recall the distinctive Fox's Gem Shop ads that ran for years in the in-flight magazine. The ads were infectious. In fact, Alaska customers became so attached to the familiar columns that when the ad stopped running, they actually took the time to voice their disappointment, many going so far as to send letters of protest to the upscale shop on Seattle's fashionable Fifth Avenue.

Featuring a photo of the shop's dashing owner, whose twinkling eyes upstaged even his appealing smile, the ads flew in the face of conventional advertising wisdom. They were not short, sweet, and to the point. They were copy-heavy harangues about the trials and frustrations of turning one's business over to the younger generation, specifically a son-in-law who just didn't "get" how to run a fine jewelry shop. It's a truly foxy use of story that the shop's owner, Sidney Thal, masterfully executed for years.

Seattle advertising legend David Stern, a now-retired advertising consultant, originated the unusual approach to promoting an elegant jewelry store. When Thal's daughter Joy and her husband, Chai Mann, became involved in the business in 1980, Stern wrote an ad for the guest informant publication distributed to downtown hotels. It told the story of the Thal family from one generation to the next. "It went against all the rules of advertising," Chai Mann says. "It was too long and you had to read through the whole thing, but people loved it. People who had never been customers came into the shop and told us, 'We had to see who these people are!' We used that ad for years."

In the early 1990s, Mann says, "We were looking for a campaign, and David had the idea of writing an ad with Sid bitching about his son-in-law because I wanted to wear tennis shoes to work and wasn't wearing a tie. The new generation! But despite my more casual image, business had never been better.

"We enjoyed the first ad, which was very funny, so David wrote several more in a similar vein. Then, one day, Sid woke up and said, 'I can do this!' And he continued to write them himself. It worked well for Sid because, although he wasn't retired, he wasn't actively running the business anymore. He could have fun remembering old stories, and it gave Sid and me a lot to talk about, reminiscing."

The approach also worked well because it was so believable. Noted for his elegant clothing, Thal cut a dashing figure. He always dressed his long, lean frame in a three-piece suit, topped off with a flowing mustache, white hair, and a black bowler. As described by *The Seattle Times* after his death in 2002 at age 92, "At a time when Seattle was still considered a backwater town, Sidney Thal was the picture of Continental elegance." That was especially true when, as often happened, he was seen stepping out of his personal trademark—a 1954 black Austin that was an original London taxi, complete with right-side steering wheel. That car was his transportation to the store and to events around town, including tailgate parties at University of Washington football games.

Mann, on the other hand, believed more casual attire was appropriate for the times and, more to the point, the younger generation of customers. "I was always the son-in-law," Mann laughs. Thal's humorous protests described a perplexing creature who had invaded his business and taken control. One was headlined, "Why My Son-in-Law Made Me Advertising Manager." When Mann placed the ads in *Alaska Airlines* magazine and another magazine published by a prestigious downtown athletic club, their popularity grew.

"Whenever I skipped a month of advertising," Mann says, "we got calls and letters from people wondering where it was. They actually said, 'Alaska Air should be paying you to run these!' or 'It's the only thing I read.' And others said, 'It's the best thing in the magazine!'"

The ads reflected the warm, down-to-earth approach that had been winning over Fox's customers for years. After buying the 36-year-old store in 1948, Sid Thal and his wife, Berta, immediately began building a loyal following; their jewelry shop in the heart of downtown Seattle is well known and highly respected by several generations of Seattleites and families far beyond Washington state. Their approach was to get to know people on a personal level. No pretense. No guile. Just simple, down-home friendliness offering the best-quality products.

Today employees are carefully selected to ensure that they match that style. "We tell them about us—the family and the history," Mann explains. "We also use stories when we talk about the different vendors whose products we carry because we've been with them for so many years. Everybody wants a personal connection." He illustrates the point by relating a story about one couple who walked into the store looking for watches, which represent a big part of Fox's business.

"Many of our watch customers are in the high-tech industry, and they know more about the products than we do," Mann says, "because they thoroughly research everything on the Internet. So I asked this couple, 'Why would you buy from us when you can get it for less on the Web?'

"They said, 'You tell us the answer.' Because you want to talk to a real person? I asked. 'Yes!' they said."

Known in the marketing profession as relationship building, Fox's approach is not simply about technique; that would, quite literally, miss the *heart* of the matter. "I hire people who are heartfelt," Mann explains, "and hope they can learn the jewelry business. We don't want knowledgeable salespeople who sell a lot but don't connect on a heart level. They're not for us.

"We want salespeople who connect with their customers and the vendors through stories of who they are, what's important to them, and what's going on in their lives. We want our sales staff to connect as human beings so they can talk to customers about their families without worrying about selling something. We want the store to be like a living room where people are comfortable just getting to know one another."

As part of the employee training, "We share stories among the staff about employees who have been here a long time and have developed a customer base by offering whatever kind of help is needed. Someone who wants something simple, such as a new earring backing, will become a customer later if treated well."

"When people want to find a jeweler they can trust, especially for something as important as repairing their mother's jewelry," Mann says, "they ask for referrals, and many new customers tell us that they've been referred to Fox's by as many as four or five people they asked for recommendations. They often tell us they were told, 'If you want it done well, you need to go to Fox's.'"

The product mix has changed over the years, according to Mann. Fox's now sells more bridal jewelry and watches than 20 years ago, more simple bands and small stones for first marriages, and fewer large stones for second marriages. But the core values are the same. Fox's customer relationships are based on old-fashioned, personalized service, with employees demonstrating a sincere desire to find the engagement ring or watch or earrings that fits each customer's needs—and pocketbook.

Warm, friendly service reflects the owners' values, and it's not only distinctive but memorable. It's an approach that's more than a little foxy—in the very best sense. And their stories continue to spread the word.

For more on the Fox's Gem Shop story, go to www.foxsgemshop.com.

9

Northwestern Mutual: Doing The Right Thing Quietly Communicates Values Loudly

Just two years after Northwestern Mutual was established in Milwaukee, Wisconsin, as a life insurance company, a train hit a cow, derailed, and killed two policyowners. Death claims totaled $3,500; the fledgling company's assets were only $2,000. The president was faced with a critical decision: pay the full benefits or reduce them proportionately with cash on hand. To him the choice was clear. He borrowed the difference and paid the full amount due to beneficiaries.

That was in 1859, and this first legend of exceptional ethics at "The Quiet Company" is one that employees still enjoy telling. Capturing the company's core values through vignettes is, in fact, a 115-year-old company tradition. As Ted Strupp, Director of Organizational Communications, says, "It gives people a sense of being part of a company that treasures what we've learned from the past...what our values are...examples of how we've lived those values. The people here still tell stories about the first CEO as though it were yesterday. They compare the behavior of all the CEOs we've had…to see if they all have adhered to our core values.

"There are legendary stories of how our executives have handled different situations. When Don Schuenke was Chairman, he was scheduled to be interviewed by a national publication on a day that the stock market dropped sharply. The reporter was to have shadowed Schuenke for the day, and people here thought the interview should be canceled. But he told them, 'No, we're not going to behave any differently whether this reporter is here or not.' He saw it as an opportunity to show that, even in difficult situations, everyone's behavior would demonstrate our commitment to our values."

A challenging situation like that puts a company to the test. A major tragedy, such as a natural disaster, takes a big toll on an insurance/financial services firm and, in particular, its financial representatives, whose clients often are personal friends. In the September 11, 2001, terrorist attacks on the U.S., more than 150 Northwestern Mutual (NM) policyowners lost their lives. The company's financial representatives, like most of the world, reacted initially with horror and grief; then they intensified their usual top-flight personal service to do what they could to help the survivors.

Like most 37-year-olds, agent Rob Slocum's bosom buddy of 20 years never thought he was going to die young. Neither did Slocum. To his deep sorrow, however, Al Qaeda terrorists put the lie to that assumption when his friend died in Tower One of New York's World Trade Center (WTC) with no insurance and no financial plan.

"Shame on me for not having spoken to him about it," Slocum acknowledged sadly at a meeting of Northwestern Mutual financial representatives later that Fall, when he remembered his buddy and four other clients who were killed in the attacks. All were his generation. All were close friends. All were dead at the hands of terrorists.

As other financial representatives took turns sharing their losses, everyone listened quietly. Doug Miller lost his college roommate and best friend. Tom Ferry had 25 clients who had worked in the WTC; seven died. Elisa Hecht lost nine friends and associates, and 11 more perished before they could finalize the life insurance applications she had helped them put in motion. But no one lost as many clients as Sean D'Arcy, and one of them was a close friend.

The day had started just like any other, with D'Arcy admiring the unobstructed view from his office on the 41st floor of the Chrysler Building. Suddenly it became a day unlike any other. D'Arcy stood transfixed as the first plane plunged into Tower One, followed by the second plane's trajectory into Tower Two, and he watched in horror as each tower collapsed. One of his close friends worked in the WTC. D'Arcy's first reaction was shock; his second was doing the right thing for his friend's family. Less than a week before, he had reminded his friend and his wife to pay their term life insurance premium; D'Arcy instinctively dialed their phone number even before he called his own family to confirm they were OK. His friend's wife answered. She said they hadn't paid it yet, so D'Arcy told her to write a check and he'd pick it up as soon as he could get out of the city.

Easier said than done. Curb-to-curb people surged uptown. At 42nd and Park, a frustrated D'Arcy searched for a non-barricaded entrance to Grand Central Station and caught a train north to Westchester County. He drove straight to his friend's house, where his friend's wife, her family, and their friends sat outside in lawn chairs waiting for news. "One look at her told me both of us knew he was gone," D'Arcy says. Battling his emotions, he urged her to write the check, then drove it to a FedEx center. Only then did he rush to pick up his own family waiting at the children's school.

When he got home, D'Arcy discovered the government had grounded all planes, so he called his friend's wife again and had her wire a backup duplicate payment to Northwestern Mutual's home office. He spent the rest of the afternoon calling the homes of other clients who worked in the Twin Towers and surrounding buildings.

In Milwaukee, a senior management committee gathered an hour after the disaster and, by midmorning—without debate—the nation's largest individual life insurer, with three million policyowners and assets of $103 billion, had laid out a plan for helping policyowners. The committee decided they wouldn't invoke war exclusions or contest claims without solid reasons to do so, and they would accept nontraditional evidence of death rather than require death certificates. Further, they would immediately send SWAT teams of their best claims people to New York and Washington to speed payments to victims and their families. Within a day, they had reworked NM's Web site to make online claims applications easier. Remaining true to its professed values at every step of the process, the company paid benefits totaling $125 million and did it in record time: an average of five days.

It was a track record even a seasoned veteran like CEO Edward J. Zore found amazing. "We're going to pay out a lot of money," Zore told the news media shortly after the tragedy. "That's what we're in business to do. We will do the right thing."

What struck Zore most on his visit to claims offices hurriedly set up at Ground Zero was that NM financial representatives whose clients filed claims showed a sense of pride, a sense of purpose. "They recognized more than ever that what they do is vital. I heard it in their voices and saw it in their eyes. I saw a resolve not to just carry on, but to do more. I heard a renewed commitment to their profession and their calling.

"Being with our financial representatives at this time was one of the most moving experiences of my life. I have never been prouder of our people, and of how important our business is to people in need."

The tragedy significantly altered the way all NM financial representatives prospect for, approach, and work with most clients. It gave them a newfound sense of urgency for helping people move forward with decisions that tend to get postponed. As he worked on the WTC claims, Sean D'Arcy found that some of his clients didn't have adequate coverage, and he resolved to do an even better job of convincing policyowners to have full protection.

Elisa Hecht agreed. Heartbroken that her friends weren't sufficiently covered or had procrastinated until it was too late, she said her experience has enabled her to more effectively meet customers' needs. "Now I can share my experience with my prospects because it will come from my heart," she says.

Northwestern Mutual Financial Network videotaped many of the stories that financial representatives shared about their clients who were killed on 9/11. D'Arcy's and Hecht's were among them. Many similar experiences were shared in e-mail messages and other company communications, following a long-held tradition of sharing stories to motivate one another to make a difference in someone's life. The aftereffects of 9/11 somberly underscored the representatives' need to share personalized stories and also reminded them that they needed to hear others'. The objective was to encourage representatives to redouble their commitment to the first—and most important—of Northwestern Mutual's five core values: doing what's right for policyowners.

The message was emphasized repeatedly at every level as people struggled to cope with personal losses. Bill Beckley, Executive Vice President of Agencies, reassured the financial representatives in a company newspaper story that "what we do is a very noble and very important thing for our clients." Philadelphia-based David Hilton, Jr., counseled his fellow representatives in Northwestern Mutual's daily online newsletter to use the tragedy to create urgency—not in clients but in themselves. "We need to visualize the financial troubles families not covered may have to endure."

Mark Lucius, Director of Corporate Information, points out, "Few jobs allow you to see the direct results of your work as sales does. It's a very one-on-one human relations business. The better our representatives can explain our values, as exemplified by these stories, to our policyowners, the better they understand the values themselves."

Official "keeper of the stories," Wesley focuses on vignettes that remind people of the company's character and values. All NM executives are designated keepers of the culture, which, Wesley says, encircles everyone. "Once you see it and experience it by working here, you begin to notice how it's expressed through employee behavior and dedication and longevity. We treat each other with a great deal of respect, and that is an outgrowth of the value system that has been in place for 147 years.

"Storytelling has always been a part of us and we're proud of our culture. When you manage through stories, you bring people in; it's interesting, it's motivating, and it's real. We still pay attention to the individual…and our culture feels like a family."

Proud employees display an almost religious devotion to excellence that sets NM apart from its competitors. Fred Harmon, Garry Jacobs, and Frederick G. Harmon, authors of *The Vital Difference: Unleashing the Powers of Sustained Corporate Success*, write, "A harmony exists between the company's employees, its field agents, and policyowners...the harmony of a close-knit family that believes what it is doing is good." What's most impressive about Northwestern Mutual, according to the authors and editor Peter F. Drucker, is how the company continues to translate its highest ideals into daily practice. Service, which Northwestern Mutual defines through its core value of "doing the right thing for the policyowner," isn't imposed from the top down. Rather, the authors assert, it is an attitude imbued in the company's personality, an attitude that influences how all employees think about and execute their work. Northwestern Mutual is "a place where the value is actually internalized by the employees as a personal belief and commitment in their own lives."

The strength of its employees' belief and devotion is in no small part due to the company's long-held commitment to integrity, which is clearly expressed in its original 72-word creed, unchanged since 1888, as well as the stories that live on. Integrity is clearly shown in the recent example of a student pilot whose policy had a standard clause—an aviation exclusion specifying that no benefits would be paid if he died in a flying accident while training to be a pilot or crew member. Less than three years after taking out the policy, he was killed while flying a plane that crashed. The flight log found in the wreckage showed that, during the trip, he had completed the 100 flying hours needed to qualify as a pilot. Although he hadn't been able to notify the company that he had met the requirements to remove the exclusion, Northwestern Mutual paid on the policy.

Northwestern Mutual's core advertising message is also more than just a slogan; it amplifies the company's values with clarity: "Integrity, financial strength, and building enduring relationships is what The Quiet Company is all about." The company's enduring commitment to these values is demonstrated by a remarkable achievement: earning a spot—not once or twice or 10 times, but 20 times—on *Fortune* magazine's list of "America's Most Admired Companies." Northwestern Mutual has also been named as one of its industry's globally "Most Admired" four consecutive times.

During a period when the public's faith in business ethics has been rocked repeatedly by tales of greed, corruption, and outright thievery at the highest corporate levels, Northwestern Mutual has maintained the highest ratings from all four major rating agencies: Standard & Poor's, A.M. Best, Fitch Ratings, and Moody's. No wonder CEO Zore is pleased to point out, "Everybody here is trying to do the right thing. We've got our moral compass in the right direction."

Due to a less-restrictive regulatory environment, the Northwestern Mutual Financial Network and other companies once limited to insurance can now extend their services to include investment specialists, security brokers and trust advisers. Virtually every financial institution, from banks to brokerage houses to insurance companies, is focused on capturing part of the $10-14 trillion that aging parents are expected to leave to their children over the next 20 years. While this change presents opportunities, it also has the potential of disrupting a company's mission and adversely affecting morale and motivation, especially if the leadership team fails to align new objectives with existing values. Keeping this in mind as they started to retool the business and adapt the brand to a widening range of services, Zore and the Northwestern Mutual management team found, to their delight, a reassuring depth of loyalty among employees.

"From policyowners to employees to the field force, everybody was on the same page. Everyone believes that this company does the right thing. No one around here is out to make a quick buck or take advantage of someone else. Everyone is just trying to do the best job they can and deliver quality products and services. That's the Northwestern Mutual brand," Zore says.

Deanna Tillisch says the branding project spanned two years "because we didn't want to cannibalize the center of what we stood for." As a result, today's core story is much the same as when the company began, despite numerous acquisitions, setting up new ways of doing business, and establishing new entities under the Northwestern Mutual umbrella. "We've preserved the tradition and built from that base," Tillisch continues. "Our CEOs come from within, so outsiders aren't coming into the company with their own agendas."

Ted Strupp agrees that the legends and lore of an organization should not be lost. "When our executive officers retire, they are interviewed by a historian so we can capture their experiences. We value the stories they tell.

"We also promote longevity. We like to keep people who know how we like to do business, so we try to show them that they're part of a long-term relationship. We do that by talking about traditions and history; it gives them the sense of being part of an organization that values what we've learned from the past…and makes people comfortable being part of a great institution. What holds us together are the people and the stories, and that's something we prize."

NM's belief in people and their stories is borne out by the remarkably low turnover rate among the 4,400 employees at corporate headquarters in Milwaukee. More than 1,000 workers there have been with the company over 20 years, and nearly twice as many have been there longer than 10 years. Their accumulated experience enhances the company's competitive advantage. As Tillisch notes, "People don't leave companies; they leave managers. So we want to create an environment where they have the autonomy and support to do their jobs well."

The company left no doubt of that support in 2001 when, facing the effects of terrorist acts and a dot-com meltdown, companies across America cut more than 1.5 million workers and reduced benefits for many remaining on the payroll. Not The Quiet Company.

"Because of mutuality, we don't have to lop off heads just to meet some quarterly earnings targets," CEO Zore explains. "We don't have to worry about earnings per share and stock performance. People know us as the ultimate mutual company, and we love that distinction." Good benefits help, too. Zore says, "While other companies are cutting back on health care choices and benefits, we've made our package even better." And, according to Kushner & Co., Inc., a benefits consulting group, NM's pensions are generous enough to earn a high ranking in the insurance industry.

The results of treating people well, Strupp says, "are people who work more productively and efficiently and who make wise decisions. They can do things right the first time. That's the payoff! Those are the metrics we value, and those are all measurable effects of stories. But of course, stories aren't the only factor that influences those outcomes."

Northwestern Mutual has collected a wealth of anecdotes over the years, and tales about the heroic work of one loyal employee in particular could fill a book. John Filak, project specialist in the controller's department, hunts through Social Security death records, lists of former employers, and any other clues he can uncover to search for "lost" policyowners. He primarily looks for people 75 or older who have lost contact with the company—and he tracks down an average of 275 every year!

In one successful hunt, the super sleuth was having trouble finding public records on a 97-year-old policyowner. Filak decided to phone the man's former employer, whose last contact had been with the insured's son while he was serving in the Peace Corps in the 1960s. After many starts and stops, Filak tracked the son down in Central America, where he was still living. His father had recently moved into a nursing care facility in the U.S., he told Filak, and he was overjoyed to learn that his father's medical policy would help defray nursing home costs and gratified that the coverage would help with eventual funeral expenses.

Stories like that stir the heart and help attract new employees to Northwestern Mutual's ranks. Recruiting is one of the foremost responsibilities assigned to financial representatives, and yet, retaining and growing their own ranks—currently 7,900 strong—can be a challenge. Competitors are constantly trying to lure away the company's sales team, which *Sales & Marketing* magazine continually honors among the nation's best.

Even more difficult is recruiting an employee population that mirrors the growing diversity of prospective customers. "With knowledge and skill being equal, diverse markets prefer a representative from their own culture...someone they feel comfortable with, someone they can communicate with and trust," says Babette Honore, Assistant Director of Multicultural/Emerging Markets. To diversify the employee population, financial representatives now target college interns, Asian Indians, African Americans, and women (currently 22% of the team). Corporate media support the effort by featuring stories of exceptional service to people in those populations.

Once the right people are recruited and become loyal employees, they generate equally loyal customers. Only 4% of Northwestern Mutual customers switch providers in any year—half the industry average—and policyowners usually stay with the company 40 years. Zore says, "This retention rate lets us have more of their money to invest longer, while spending less to replace defectors. Savings are used to lower prices or deploy more field reps.

"What we've seen in the wake of the terrorist attacks is a reawakening to our core principles in the marketplace...a return to the really important things, but with more urgency than I've ever seen." For Zore himself, the importance of being prepared became a personal reality several years before the terrorist attacks. To drive home the message, he shared a story at the company's Eastern Regional Conference early in 2002 about his own close brush with death.

The story unfolded on the same day that an electrician finished installing an automatic boat winch at Zore's vacation cottage. Zore and his wife, Diane, were playing fetch down by the lake with their chocolate Labrador retriever, Clyde. The dog disappeared around the boathouse, a stick clenched in his mouth, but didn't return. Zore said, "Diane yelled, and I ran into the lake to look for the dog. I saw him under about two feet of water, spread over the steel rails that guide the boat out of the lake. When I reached to grab him, I froze in the same electrical field that had paralyzed Clyde. Diane came over to grab me. I could barely talk, but yelled at her not to touch me. As I stood there, both arms in the water, I remember feeling the life draining out of me...from my head down through my body and out of my feet."

Frantic, Diane grabbed a broom and knocked one of her husband's arms out of the water. He was able to snag the broomstick, and she pulled him to shore. After Diane turned off the circuit breakers, they dragged Clyde out of the water. Zore pumped his chest while Diane breathed into his muzzle, and the dog finally showed signs of life. "When we got Clyde to the vet, she called it a miracle," Zore continued. "Then she took a closer look at me and said, 'I think the dog will be fine, but you look horrible.' She was right. I was gaunt...my face gray.

"The story has a happy ending, though. Clyde's been a little goofy since the accident, but he's still with us...and still a great bird dog. And, for a while, my assistant noticed my penmanship improved...but that didn't last!"

On a more serious note, he said that facing his own mortality made him much more interested in securing a solid financial position for his own family. "I now have the coverage I need. In fact, I probably have five times the coverage I need."

Not surprisingly, the CEO of The Quiet Company exemplifies Northwestern Mutual's core values: integrity, financial strength, loyalty to employees, loyalty to policyowners, going the extra mile, and believing that what you do changes people's lives. And the results of such actions are loudly evidenced in the bottom line. Over the past 10 years, the Northwestern Mutual team nearly tripled the company's life insurance in force—from $250 billion to more than $750 billion—and more than doubled its annual dividend payout. In 2002 and again in 2003, dividends set records while premiums remained relatively flat, a performance that far outpaced the industry. Edward Zore predicts that future performance will be even better.

"What holds us together," Deanna Tillisch explains, "is the intangible value in the power of people and their stories. We don't produce a widget. Our product is really the human story—how we affect people: employees, policyowners, the field force, suppliers. We make certain our stories are consistent for all these audiences."

For more information on the Northwestern Mutual story, go to www.nwfm.com.

10

FedEx: Shoot. Move. Communicate. And Deliver The Beans

Whether heading a large corporation or a five-person shop, an inspiring leader must communicate the company's objectives to all the stakeholders, marshal the forces to support its mission, and possess the stick-to-it-iveness to breathe life into its goals with continuous reinforcement and rewards.

On all counts, FedEx Corporation Chairman, President, and CEO Fred Smith fills that bill. If he didn't possess those qualities, plus a knowledge of what makes employees tick and keeps customers happy, his business might never have gotten off the ground. Pursuing his vision with dogged determination, he has inspired a loyal following of corporate troops by adopting the technique he learned as a Marine in Vietnam: communicating in brief, to-the-point messages. Adding his own twist, Smith often wraps his messages in stories. The practice is so entrenched in the FedEx culture that almost every employee can tell you how Smith got his start.

After earning a bachelor's degree from Yale, he spent 13 months as a Marine rifle platoon leader and company commander in Vietnam. That's where he got the best leadership advice of his life, he told a *Harvard Business Review* roundtable. A young Marine lieutenant told him the secret behind every good troop leader: "Just remember three things: Shoot. Move. Communicate."

Smith says the shoot and move rules translate to decisiveness in the corporate world, and he amplifies that directive with another military metaphor: "Pick a target and go for it and don't stand still to make an easy target for your enemies." As for the third part of the young lieutenant's directive, communicate, Smith explains that if leaders see employees as the ally rather than the enemy, "They'll realize the best way to look after your people is to keep them informed, even if you have to deliver bad news."

Vietnam service also taught Smith how front-line people think and what they want. He learned that, when people join an organization, they simply want their leader to answer a few straightforward questions: What do you expect from me? What's in it for me? Where do I go if I have a problem? How am I doing? Is what I'm doing important? "Providing answers is what managers do," Smith says.

In 1971, obsessed with the business value of time and the pursuit of speed, Smith founded FedEx in Little Rock, Arkansas. He based the company on a concept of overnight delivery that he had outlined in a Harvard MBA paper. His professor didn't like the idea, but Smith was not deterred.

It took two years to set up the transportation system he envisioned. In the early days, 389 FedEx employees used their own cars, a small fleet of rented vans, and 14 Falcon jets to pick up and drop off packages in 25 U.S. cities. Legend has it that Xerox was so skeptical, they tested the system with empty boxes before they would entrust Smith's brainchild with real packages. Despite his professor's and his prospective customers' doubts, Smith quickly proved his concept. He is now Chairman of a holding company that employs more than 218,000 people, provides service to 215 countries, and delivers approximately 5.4 million packages a day.

"He ran into enormous roadblocks and never gave up," a woman named Ellen wrote in an unsolicited message posted on www.FastCompany.com. "What he did took enormous courage and persistence. The guy is a visionary of the highest magnitude. This country is great because of its trailblazers, and he's one of them."

"Stories about the company's beginnings are still powerful," says Shirlee Clark, Director of Corporate Communications, noting that company leaders make a point to tell new stories all the time. We replicate stories as many times and in as many ways as we can—through internal communications, speeches, and a whole host of ways. You name it, we use it." Internally, FedEx uses an intranet, an Internet-based TV network, and Web sites employees can access, as well as news initiatives, face-to-face meetings, print publications, and audiotapes that over-the-road drivers can listen to.

"We try to find what works best with each work group to target our messages," Clark continues. "For example, the sales force wants to hear from senior executives about new initiatives and company direction, so we use electronic communication—posting information many times daily on our Web site and using short video-on-demand segments—because Sales tells us that's most convenient and effective for them. Subsequent research has confirmed that's the case." That's just a small sampling of how the company enacts the mantra, Shoot. Move. Communicate.

"Generally speaking, though, storytelling works best in either broadcast media [video/Webcast] or print. You have more space and time to develop the story," Clark explains. "Anecdotes that reemphasize our culture are the most effective. Many of our hero stories are legendary. They've become institutionalized, and everyone's aware of them."

Anyone who doubts Clark's assertion might be persuaded by asking any local FedEx courier about the early days when executives pawned their watches to buy gas to keep company vehicles running. More to the point, a skeptic might ask that same employee to share *his or her* favorite story. One woman who tested the company's story culture discovered that everyone at her local FedEx office had a different tale to tell, and many remembered one from the most recent company videotape they had seen: when a top exec appeared in golf shirt, heavy gloves, and steel-toed boots to sweat alongside other employees at the Memphis hub to handle the additional one million pounds of packages a day received during a UPS strike. Or when FedEx supersized its cargo business to transport whales between Sea Worlds in Japan and San Diego.

Many FedEx stories center on winners of the Purple Promise Award, which comes with a sizeable check. Presented at a special ceremony, the award represents individual employees' single-minded commitment to their company and their communities, and it recognizes unselfish acts that enhance customer service. In one case in Puerto Rico, a FedEx delivery truck broke down and its driver convinced the tow truck operator to take her to her last delivery of the day, complete with FedEx truck in tow.

Joe Kinder is another Purple Promise winner. The Buffalo, New York, courier heard about a couple on his route waiting for an envelope containing visas so they could go to Russia. They were trying to adopt a little boy before the threatened closure of adoptions to foreigners in a few days. When the visas didn't arrive, Kinder tracked down the misaddressed package and went miles out of his way to hand-deliver it to the couple.

When his FedEx van died in 90° Colorado heat, Steven Schott borrowed a customer's bicycle, strapped packages to his back, and pedaled 10 miles up and down the steep foothills of Boulder, Colorado, to complete his deliveries on time. He's proud of his award. So is Tyler Perkins, who displayed FedEx pride in Montana, where he delivers packages during the day and breaks horses after work. In Big Sky Country, horses tend to get loose now and then, so Perkins carries a halter in his van with his name and address attached. When he finds a horse outside a fence, he slips the halter on the animal, ties the horse to a tree or post, and continues on his route. The horse's owner always mails the halter back, often with a thank-you note.

FedEx also loves to disseminate stories about its own Humanitarian honorees, who also are recognized at the Purple Promise ceremony. One award cited an employee for saving a toddler walking down a busy highway. Another recognized the heroism of a courier for reviving a nearly drowned child in a backyard swimming pool by following an EMS dispatcher's directions. Another honored 10-year FedEx veteran Eddie Heussler, who suffered second- and third-degree burns to 45% of his body while trying in vain to rescue a 79-year-old woman from her burning Virginia home. After a brave year-long fight, Eddie recovered from his injuries and returned to work. A local police captain wrote to the company, describing Eddie's efforts as "beyond exceptional" and vowing that his actions would never be forgotten.

Another recognition, the Bravo Zulu Award, is given for efforts above and beyond the call of duty and often is tied to a specific project or event. Both the individual and team awards create a lot of pride as well as peer pressure. As Clark says, "It's contagious."

Regularly recognizing and celebrating "heroes" ensures that each of FedEx's employees is clear on the corporate mission. Motivating them to work at their peak levels to fulfill the mission, not just do the bare minimum to avoid getting fired, is another part of a manager's role, Chairman Fred Smith points out. "To constantly reinforce the organization's vision and values, our primary tool is to share the rewards," Smith wrote. Leonard L. Berry, author of *Discovering the Soul of Service*, concurs, noting that most people want to do the right thing; they just need to be rewarded for it.

Rewards at FedEx start with good pay and benefits for everyone. Most part-time employees get the same benefits as full-timers, including partially paid health coverage and good pensions. Appropriately, the company reserves its largest financial incentives for its most critical core value: extraordinary customer service. But financial rewards are only part of the story.

An "unfailing respect for people" is another of the rewards at FedEx. It's one way a leader inspires the kind of performance FedEx employees are known for, says Executive Vice President and Chief Information Officer Rob Carter. He obviously knows what he's talking about, having repeatedly earned industry recognition as an outstanding leader.

Not surprisingly, respect builds loyalty. One FedEx manager posted a message on www.FastCompany.com to point out that, while his excellent IT skills make him employable just about anywhere, he's still at FedEx because of the basic principles Fred Smith has been teaching for years. "They flow throughout the entire company, from courier to pilot to professional," he wrote. "As a result, getting up and going to work every day is exciting. FedEx has taught me so many valuable skills that not only apply to work, but to my personal life as well. The leadership program made me aware of leadership characteristics I already possessed and taught me to enhance them further. Both my career and raising my new son have benefited from my learning experiences at FedEx."

Additional evidence of a well-led company is low employee turnover. And when openings become available, there are plenty of eager candidates. Noted for its hiring practices, FedEx mirrors the diversity of its customer base.

Minorities represented 40% and women 28% of the workforce in 2003, earning the company a spot again on *Fortune's* "Best Companies for Minorities" list.

FedEx has measured employee-motivation levels on a regular basis for more than 25 years. As students in Business 101 learn, what gets measured gets managed, and "What we're really measuring is leadership," Smith told HBR roundtable participants. "When people say an organization failed because of a lack of leadership, they usually mean its leaders were unable to reinforce the types of activities that lead to success and unable to quit doing the things that don't.

"If our employees are happy and our customers are happy, those are signs the company's leadership is communicating the vision and values correctly and rewarding them appropriately. That's a great competitive advantage in a service business like FedEx where the value chain is outside the four walls."

By all measures, FedEx's customers are as happy as its employees. A leading provider of global transportation, e-commerce, and supply-chain business and management services, the company reported record earnings in 2003 of $22.5 billion (up 9% from the previous year). And FedEx is close to the top on customer satisfaction. Internet-based Harris Interactive in Rochester, New York, surveyed more than 60,000 consumers of goods from 150 companies to measure the companies' placement in five categories: emotional appeal, products and services, financial performance, vision and leadership, workplace environment, and social responsibility. FedEx ranked eighth. The company also received United Way's Spirit of America Award in 2003, as well as three of the four Summit Awards the year before (for employee campaigns, major gifts, and volunteer programs).

Other signs that the company's approach works are the honors it receives from the business world. FedEx's numerous awards include being named to "Best Companies" and "Best Employers" lists worldwide, among them *Forbes'* "Platinum 400 Best Big Companies in America" in 2003. The company has been one of *Fortune's* "100 Best Companies to Work For" since its inception, has placed in the top 10 of *Fortune's* "America's Most Admired Companies" several years in a row, and was honored as a *Fortune* "Blue Ribbon Company" for appearing on six of the magazine's honor lists in 2003, including the "Global 500" and "Global Most Admired." In addition, Smith was one of *Forbes'* "Top CEOs" in 2001.

"Most companies on the Fortune 100 have fewer than 50,000 employees, making it all the more amazing we rank so high," Clark says with pride.

CFO magazine's Russ Banham once dubbed overnight delivery "an improbable idea, with an unattainable public goal" (Absolutely, Positively) and "a laudable internal motto" (People, Service, Profit). But FedEx now reaches virtually 100% of U.S. homes, and Banham, like other doubters, has been proven wrong.

Bringing the e-world together with the real world is what his company does better than anyone else, Smith claims. FedEx has combined its physical, information, and people networks and has invested about $1.5 billion a year in the most sophisticated information technology and IT people to bring Internet speed to the business. The result: FedEx customers now generate more than two million shipments each day with automated transactions. Those shipments and millions of others are handled by a ground fleet of 70,000 motorized vehicles and an airfleet of 643.

Before the economic slowdown after the turn of the century, Boston-based Gartner Research predicted worldwide B-2-B commerce would reach $8.5 trillion worldwide by 2005. FedEx is positioned to take advantage of that growth.

In his quest to follow the soldier's creed of "Lead, follow, or get the hell out of the way," Smith continues to push for 10% overall annual revenue growth, and envisions that FedEx profits will rise at an even faster clip. In the meantime, when he gets on an airplane or meets people for the first time, Smith is prepared to hear a story, generally about a time a FedEx employee saved the day. Clark experiences the same satisfaction. "Because we encourage every one of our 219,000 ambassadors to be friendly, innovative, positive, and helpful, we clearly know the business we're in, and so do our customers."

Gerry Holland sure knows what business *he's* in.With threatening weather closing in, the Purple Promise Award winner called his Cookville, Tennessee, customer from a corner market prior to delivering a package. He wanted to know about driving conditions to her house on a narrow road on the side of a bluff two miles from the main road. She advised him not to attempt the drive. If he *did* decide to come, however, would he bring her three cans of beans from the market? Holland braved the weather to trudge up and down hills to the customer's house to deliver the FedEx Overnight Letter. And an order of beans.

There's no doubt in Holland's mind, or the minds of his fellow employees, about FedEx's mission and how they can help fulfill it. They know the story of Smith's inspiration, they're familiar with legends of the early days, and they continually hear tales about coworkers' heroic accomplishments. "Shoot. Move. Communicate." Holland knew that directive meant to deliver the beans.

For more information on the FedEx story, go to www.fedex.com.

11

WRQ:
Just Like Racing A Bike

Most people wouldn't expect to see a cyclist on the cover of a software company's annual report, but anyone familiar with WRQ wouldn't be surprised. The close-up photo of a cyclist's feet and the brief story superimposed on it epitomize WRQ's corporate culture. Comparing the company to world-class bicycle racers, the introduction states, "Those who succeed are well trained and race proven. They have an overwhelming desire to win—a desire fueled by confidence, teamwork, endurance, and commitment. WRQ shares the same overwhelming desire to win."

Inside the cover, the theme continues with an unusually casual photo accompanying the Chairman's letter. Instead of the expected shot depicting a formally posed executive wearing a business suit and a weighty expression, Chairman, CEO and founding partner Doug Walker is wearing bright yellow cycling gear and a big grin. Following his name and title, the caption includes the description, "daily cyclist since 1981," the year Walker and his partners founded WRQ. He's been riding his bike to work every day since, just as many employees do.

"We have more bicycle riders percentage-wise than REI," Walker laughs, as he describes WRQ's casual, activity-oriented culture. A member of REI's Board of Directors, he's quick to point out that one reason for that is WRQ's central location near downtown versus REI's headquarters on the outer edge of a suburban business district. Also, at WRQ's corporate headquarters, if employees need a car during the day to run personal errands, they know they can borrow Walker's car without asking permission. "I have an extremely inexpensive car," he says, laughing again. "It doesn't even have a radio, so someone taped a picture of a radio to the dashboard! The key hangs on a hook just inside my office door with a tag on it that tells where it's parked so anyone can grab it and go." In return, everyone who uses Walker's car buys gas when needed and helps to maintain it.

That level of teamwork and ownership is no accident. Teamwork is one of WRQ's core values and underlying it, Walker says, is another: individual responsibility. These two fundamental values are emphasized continuously, beginning with employee orientation. The very first training session drives home the importance of taking responsibility for whatever needs to be done to improve operations or customer service. One of the largest privately-held software companies based in the U.S., WRQ empowers its staff of 425 to carry out that directive, beginning with the hiring process itself. "There's a key value related to how you treat people. We have a participative hiring process, so employees feel they have a stake in the outcome," Walker says. "People take a lot of ownership in who we hire, and that creates a commitment to the team. We give people a lot of challenge, a lot of independence, a lot of recognition. Our employees really like the people they work with, and they're proud of what they produce together."

WRQ's strong esprit de corps is exemplified in many different ways, especially in their enthusiastic support for storytelling. A history buff, Walker often uses stories about historical figures to convey corporate values and expectations. And because the WRQ workforce is oriented toward outdoor activities, he also shares stories about top athletes. "You have to use stories to tell people what you expect," Walker says.

"You can't just tell them to adopt a new attitude about work. The trick is to tell inspiring stories in such a way that you connect them to the individuals listening. Can they do the same thing as the hero of the story? Do they have it in them?" Recognizing that stories about people within the company are even more effective because people can see the connection to themselves more easily, the affable CEO depends on employees for workplace stories that he can retell. He shares them in weekly employee meetings at headquarters and annual gatherings that include employees from locations worldwide.

Reflecting the company's core values, most of the employee-generated stories are about people going the extra mile to solve customer problems; others tell how the company's products have improved customers' IT operations. WRQ builds software for accessing and integrating host applications, and four out of five Fortune 500 companies rely on their products daily. Because its customers run highly complicated systems, WRQ gives its service and support employees both the responsibility and the authority to own the customer's problem. As Walker says, "In the typical support situation, the customer service representative first tries to shift the problem back onto the customer and then passes the customer on to someone else. That means the caller has to start all over each time to explain the problem. It's frustrating and time consuming.

"Prospective customers, especially at very large companies, often ask, 'How quickly are you going to escalate my support call so I can get help without losing a lot of time?' We tell them escalation isn't necessary because our front-line people take care of customer problems themselves. In fact, our support engineers can actually order changes in a product, which typically is not the way it works. We assure prospective customers by telling them stories about how we've served other large customers, explaining how our support organization works, and sharing references, employee retention rates, and results."

A practice that sprang up organically, the storytelling system at WRQ usually runs itself, with each work team, including the production staff, generating their own collection of stories about their product. Because the stories they tell significantly influence outcomes, managers step in to help their teams make course corrections when necessary. Walker says their experience shows that "they need to have good stories or sales will start to slump and enthusiasm will drop."

Most of the vignettes he retells are about people exerting extraordinary influence, such as leading a team, or about individuals who quietly shape the way things are done in the company. One is about an engineer who isn't interested in being a manager but is a tireless advocate for improving methodologies. The company has adopted so many of his ideas that he has, through recommendations accumulated over time, originated the entire engineering methodology currently in use. Another is about a customer installation that involved several different products, and when a glitch occurred, it wasn't clear which product was the source of the problem. WRQ's service person discovered that another company's product was at fault. Instead of shifting responsibility to the manufacturer, he spent two weeks on the complex process of patching the product at the object level. "Our betas have always been considered better than other companies' shipped products," Walker says, "and that story illustrates our tradition of high-quality technology done by driven professionals."

The evidence bears out the claim. With more than six million users worldwide, WRQ has the highest customer-support rating in the industry. In addition, a 2002 survey conducted by NFO Prognostics reported that WRQ has the highest customer-loyalty ratings in the industry, and 74% of

WRQ customers surveyed said they intended to establish the company's products as their corporate standard. The survey was based on interviews with nearly 4,500 respondents in four countries, including more than 500 WRQ customers.

Corporate-wide storytelling is reinforced by WRQ's report protocol. Following the weekly employee meetings, where top-level managers and other employees share their experiences, meeting notes that include those stories are distributed company wide. Case studies are also shared regularly via e-mail, both as reports and as announcements. Presales engineers are required to file reports on each customer contact, and well-told stories are valued so highly that their peers grade the reports on how interesting and well written they are. Sales managers regularly send e-mails to share their team's successes with the rest of the company, detailing who was involved in the sale and what they did. And salespeople use stories in their presentations because they are far more effective than a listing of capabilities. Just as employees want to hear about their peers' successes because they can relate to them, prospective customers want to hear about other companies' experiences in the same or similar situation.

The WRQ team spirit even extends to employees' personal time. One example is a group of about 30 people at corporate headquarters who love mountain climbing. Every year they begin preparing in January for a climb of 14,410-foot Mt. Rainier. First they take a climbing course, and then they spend months in training before the expedition itself during the summer. Other special-interest groups also pursue their sports together.

Such camaraderie is one indication of the reason the company has been among the top 30 on *Fortune* magazine's "100 Best Companies to Work For" three years in a row, from 1999 to 2001. Another honor during that period came when

Ernest & Young's 2000 Entrepreneur of the Year Award committee named Walker "Master Entrepreneur." And in 2003, WRQ was a finalist in the "Best Overall Company" category of the American Business Awards.

Pointing out that the company has enjoyed an unusually long life for a software manufacturer, Walker says that IT has changed over the years. "It used to be a supportive function within an organization; now it's a central function. Everyone in a corporation is in essence an IT customer, and their external customers are, too." WRQ's products have grown larger and much more complex to meet the customers' expanding needs, and sales have followed, approaching $100 million in 2002. The company's fundamentals, however, are the same as they were at the beginning: the customer profile (IT managers), the company's business ethic (do the right thing for the customer), and the product category (host application access and integration).

"When someone asks me what we do," Walker says, "I emphasize our continuity. We've been connecting host applications to emerging technologies for more than two decades, expanding our products and services to meet customer needs. And I'm proud to say that the tenure of our technical support staff averages more than seven years, compared with an industry average of about one year, and our customer service reps turnover is about 5%, compared with an industry average of 25-30%. Overall, our company turnover is under 10%. We have a dedicated team that is driven to deliver high-end products with strong support."

It's even been said that working at WRQ is just like racing a bike.

For more about the WRQ story, go to www.wrq.com.

12

Medtronic: Dad, I Saved A Life Today

"My life was depressing," Gary Prazac begins. "At 49, I was diagnosed with Parkinson's Disease. Before long I looked like an old man, shuffling along with a cane and wearing that [deadpan facial expression] called 'Parkinson's mask.' One time I remember my legs were so spastic and useless, I was stuck inside the airport for three hours, my legs frozen, unable to move from my chair as I watched my plane take off." His voice breaks, and he pauses. "Huge doses of medications controlled the tremors, that's true, but they caused my body to writhe all over the place."

After suffering these and many other indignities over the years, Prazac says his physician finally offered him a ray of hope—a new therapy involving implantation of a Medtronic deep-brain-stimulation device. "The surgery reversed at least 10 years of...symptoms. It was literally a miracle. Not long ago, I was walking my Great Dane in the woods near home when a fellow dog-walker stopped to chat. He said he'd met my dog before, but an old man with a cane was with him then. 'Was that your father?' he asked."

Overcome by this powerful recollection, Prazac pauses to regain his composure before picking up the thread of the story. By now, there's not a dry eye in the audience. Brightening, Prazac adds, "Medtronic gave me my smile back."

Personal healing stories like Prazac's are told each December by six different patients and their physicians at

Medtronic's holiday event. They demonstrate why the 1,000 or so employees at the company's Minneapolis headquarters and the thousands more viewing the event worldwide via live videoconference or videotape delay come to work every day.

Chairman and Chief Executive Officer Art Collins, promoted to head Medtronic's leadership team in 2002 and the Board of Directors in 2003, says, "I'm very clear with internal and external constituencies, including Wall Street, that our most important gathering is not the annual meeting or the analysts' meeting. It's the holiday program, the day we come together as a family joined by a great and enduring mission—serving others."

Service to others has always been the heart of Medtronic. As Collins' predecessor, William W. George, told an audience at the Academy of Management, employees in every industry—not just the medical field—need to be part of something larger than themselves, to achieve something worthwhile. Named the Academy's 2001 Executive of the Year, George said, "If companies offer employees this sense of purpose consistently over a long period of time without deviating and without vacillating, they'll buy into the mission and go the extra mile to serve customers. But creating an organization of highly motivated people is extremely hard to duplicate. Motivation must be rooted in the intrinsic purpose of the work, not applied artificially by management or consultants."

Admitting he was challenging the conventional wisdom of the previous 25 years, George warned that "those companies…whose strategy derives solely from bottom-line considerations...will ultimately fail. If you sell your soul by abandoning the company's long-held values or its mission for short-term gain, you break the trust you've built up with employees."

In truly great organizations, long-term success depends on all levels of management continuously practicing, reinforcing, and reflecting the values most organizations in the world share: customer service, quality, integrity in business dealings, respect for employees, and good citizenship. Employees trust this type of company and believe in its purpose, according to George.

Earl E. Bakken, Medtronic's cofounder, Chairman Emeritus and the emcee who introduced Prazac and his physician at the 2000 holiday program, has practiced these truths his entire life. Retired since 1995 and living in Hawaii, Bakken returns to Minneapolis as often as possible to preside over the tradition he so lovingly started a lifetime ago. "It's hard to be the master of ceremonies because it's hard not to cry," he admitted after he'd listened to Prazac's story. (Some employees rank the gathering according to how many tissues they need during the afternoon.)

Prazac's journey to an enriched life began in the 1920s, long before he was even born. That's when Bakken, then a schoolboy, bought a ticket to the movie "Frankenstein." Electricity and the way it sparked life in the monster's inanimate body parts intrigued the young boy and led to his hobby of building robots in the basement and, later, a budding career repairing TVs and appliances.

One day a doctor asked him to try tweaking medical equipment in a local hospital's operating room. It wasn't long before he and his late brother-in-law, Palmer Hermundslie, were spending all their time inventing and developing medical devices. In 1949, they formed Medtronic and housed it in the latter's 600-square-foot garage, pot belly stove and all. It's a legend similar to the lore surrounding Bill Gates' creation of Microsoft and Bill Hewlett and Dave Packard's birthing of Hewlett-Packard.

In 1957, Bakken invented the world's first wearable, battery-powered, transistorized cardiac pacemaker. Presenting Bakken with its "Engineering for Gold" Award in 1984, the National Society of Professional Engineers called the device one of the 10 most outstanding engineering achievements in 50 years. Later Medtronic's two founders licensed the first implantable pacemaker from its designers, and the growing Medtronic team labored night and day to produce and sell it and to apply technology to other medical problems. But they were hemorrhaging capital with little in reserve, and by 1960 the money was running out.

When the future father of modern medical science tried to get a loan, the bank turned him down flat. A close counselor and friend, Tom Holloran, pointed out that bankers didn't have any idea what Medtronic did. That's all it took to send Bakken home to write "The Medtronic Mission," reapply for the loan, and get it. Bakken's pacemaker invention has since led to the development of increasingly sophisticated electronic devices credited with saving or improving the lives of millions of patients around the globe.

Not one word of the Medtronic mission has changed since Bakken wrote it, despite the fact that today it's one of America's 40 most financially valuable companies, with nearly 30,000 employees worldwide and 2003 revenues of $7.66 billion. "We're in business to apply biomedical engineering in the research, design, manufacture, and sale of products that alleviate pain, restore health, and extend life," Collins says. "We talk about that constantly. It's an extremely important part of what makes Medtronic tick."

Equally significant to the leadership team's way of thinking is that Medtronic therapies reach several million patients in more than 120 countries each year. Among them are U.S. Vice President Dick Cheney and entertainer Jerry

Lewis. Every seven seconds, the life of someone somewhere in the world is improved by a Medtronic product or therapy.

Collins is quick to credit Bakken with using the power of story and personal example to create a passion for the work, its mission and its values among employees. That's been the key to Medtronic's success.

Vice President of Executive and Leadership Development Paul Erdahl notes that "stories spread the glue of the mission throughout the organization." And 21-year company veteran Dick Ploetz, Vice President of Human Resource Systems and Operations, points to the holiday program and the Mission and Medallion Ceremony as the centers of Medtronic's story-based communications.

Every new employee is invited to attend the ceremony, where the CEO explains the company's birth, evolution, and mission, and tells about early Medtronic breakthroughs. Once a year, Earl Bakken participates in the Mission and Medallion Ceremony and shares his stories along with Collins.

One is about Bakken's contribution to the development of pacemakers. Some of the early devices were large boxes on carts, plugged into wall sockets so patients could be moved from room to room. One night a storm knocked out the electrical supply at the University of Minnesota Hospitals, and a baby on a pacemaker died. Shaken, one of the surgeons asked Bakken if Medtronic could come up with something better. He did. Bakken invented the electronic pacemaker, a truly portable, dependable unit. The rest of the story is among the collection in Bakken's book, *One Man's Full Life.*

Among the Medtronic founder's other accomplishments is the founding in 1975 of The Bakken Library and Museum in Minneapolis. A center "of electricity in life," the facility houses 11,000 rare books and 2,500 scientific instruments and includes an exhibit entitled, "Geeks, Mavericks, and Mad Scientists: Images and Reality!"

Clear-eyed leaders like Bakken and Collins know that a company's success depends on tapping into its employees' own core values and giving them a cause larger than themselves. So after the stories are told at the Mission and Medallion Ceremony, Collins hands each employee a bronze medallion and small stand. On the front of the medallion is Medtronic's logo, which features a bas-relief prone figure rising from a table Lazarus-like to a standing position, surrounded by the words: "When life depends on medical technology."

Bakken often told new employees, "There will be many times when you get frustrated with your work. When you do, look at your medallion and think about the symbol of 'the rising person.' Your work here...is not just to make money for yourself or the company, but to restore people to fuller lives."

His successors share his views, and one indication is that the leadership transitions have been seamless. After Medtronic completed five major mergers in 1998 and 1999, Bakken, George, and Collins personally conducted Mission and Medallion Ceremonies for more than 9,000 new employees in Japan, India, South Africa, virtually every European country, and many U.S. locations. Some ceremonies even occur in the middle of the night for second- and third-shift employees.

"When I speak to employee groups—small or large—I relate concepts through personal experience, which bring them to life," Collins says. "One of the most indelible ways I get into our business is when I scrub up for surgery to watch as patients receive one of our devices. I talk to those people later to find out how the devices have helped them.

"And strangers frequently come up to me to relate their gratitude for our products. Another CEO introduced himself recently at a conference to tell me he has one of our insulin pumps, and it's changed his life.

"I share those stories with employees," Collins says, "because the real strength of Medtronic is not a few people at the top. It's all 30,000 employees and their total commitment to the mission. At the end of the day, it's all about people serving physicians and their patients."

In addition to the holiday program and Mission and Medallion Ceremony, storytelling plays a significant role in other communications. The annual report features patients and their stories, as does the corporate art collection. Photos of people whose lives have been enriched, accompanied by the story of how that happened, make people proud to work where they do. "The mission is in the air everywhere you turn," Erdahl says.

To make certain Medtronic executives know the implications their decisions hold for employees and the business, selected vice presidents and senior managers attend week-long sessions for senior Medtronic leaders that focus on the company's values, ethics, and mission. That way, if a crisis occurs, it will be second nature for the leadership team to remain true to Medtronic's guiding principles.

At one of the early sessions, so the legend goes, Bakken came into the room, policy manuals handcuffed to his ankle. By the time he'd dragged the heavy three-ring binders over to the fireplace and thrown each in, one by one, he'd already taught the lesson that red tape can hamper progress. Employees were telling that one for years.

A St. Thomas University ethics expert provides the stories to facilitate the Medtronic Leader program, where 20-25 people nominated by company executives and managers spend a week discussing ethics, case studies, and other leadership issues. Personal leadership based on one's life purpose is one of the company's highest values, so participants spend up to two of those days exploring what the mission means and identifying how their own personal values and mission are aligned with it. Each person documents the resulting story for their own personal reference, and they're encouraged to share it with others. Many share their stories with their families, some with their employees.

Many of the tales spread throughout the company center on the extraordinary actions taken by members of the sales force, explains Jackie Dami, Human Resources Assistant. For example, Medtronic representatives have been known to drive hundreds of miles in the middle of the night to deliver a pacemaker to a physician. These corporate dramas haven't just filtered through employee ranks willy-nilly; leaders have made certain they're distributed worldwide.

"'What difference will you have made at the end of your career?' is a question I often think about," Collins says, "and it inspires some of the stories I tell employees. In my office I have a rocking chair to remind me that when I'm retired and sitting in that chair, and my grandchildren ask me what was important in my life, I won't tell them about extra earnings per share. Earnings are important, of course, but employees need to see their leaders as human beings. So I'll tell my grandchildren, as I tell employees, how this work has touched my own life."

In his quiet way, Bakken insisted that every employee, particularly company leaders, adhere to the customer-first commandment. "It's a commandment not always easy to obey, especially when [leaders'] days are filled with meetings, planning, developing, and executing strategy, and putting the vision into practice, but it's the most important," he wrote in *Reflections on Leadership*, a volume still used in Medtronic management training.

"Everything we do, regardless of our individual titles, ultimately is related to product sales. The tone of correspondence, the way our phone calls are answered, the friendliness of employees, even the appearance of our buildings. New employees must be instilled with this sensibility, veteran employees regularly reminded of it."

Teaching by example, Bakken carried 3 x 5 cards to record physicians' desires and personal information, such as families, hobbies, special concerns, and interests. Then he transferred the data to his computer so he could review it before making the next call to that doctor.

"Every customer of every company is important," Bakken wrote, "but Medtronic customers [physicians] are especially important. [They are] men and women of great intellect and education, [and] their technical expertise and experience is often staggering, as is their responsibility to their patients whose lives may rest, quite literally, in their hands. Their time is precious, their patience sometimes short. Independent and proud, they do not like being abandoned, slighted, or put on hold." When physicians call, Bakken advised Medtronic leaders, "You'd better instruct your secretaries to interrupt what you're doing and answer that call at their convenience, not yours."

To illustrate the damage done when employees don't listen to customers, Bakken recounts how a young, enthusiastic engineer out to dinner with a Medtronic customer couldn't wait to share his excitement about his latest project. He bent the doctor's ear from the time the salad was served until coffee and dessert arrived. At the end of the evening, the engineer knew nothing more about the doctor and his needs than he did at the beginning. Needless to say, he didn't make the sale.

Listening to the customer is, indeed, critical. So is managing the people whose dedication to an absurd idea leads to an earth-shaking innovation. Aloof, contentious, noisy, disruptive, misfit, troublemaker—all could describe those few people whose creative force sometimes makes them dazzling visionaries, ingenious engineers, or gifted scientists, and creates the stuff of legend.

Brilliant mavericks can exact a heavy toll in morale and efficiency, so uninformed managers often show them the door. That's a big mistake, Bakken writes, since "they may be the persons who can put our company ahead of the competition." Effective leaders, he adds, neither bury nonconformists nor let them venture too far off on their own.

"Managers must establish and maintain an atmosphere where new ideas, sometimes far out, sometimes radical, can be heard and examined" and use "imagination and patience to accommodate ornery thinkers. Our better managers listen, even when listening isn't easy or particularly pleasant."

Dick Ploetz concurs in this need for trust and freedom. "Some of our major businesses have resulted from small groups of people dedicated to an idea that hadn't been approved. One employee stayed with a product even after the company gave it up, and it became one of our best-selling products of all time. I'm not sure how many businesses would tolerate that."

Today Medtronic has evolved into an organization that helps physicians restore people with chronic disease to richer, fuller lives by offering products and therapies that help them solve the most challenging, life-limiting problems; improve health; extend life; and alleviate pain. Its roots in the treatment of heart disease have expanded into supporting physicians in cardiovascular; neurological; diabetes; spinal surgery; ear, nose and throat; and ophthalmology specialties. The number of potential lives Medtronic could eventually enrich is staggering.

The company's agility in adapting to the market and taking advantage of advancing technology means it's had to reinvent itself every five years. Yet its people have never lost sight of the mission and core values because they are reinforced regularly through stories. The Medtronic passion for learning, discovery, and innovation, and the corporate team's commitment to the best product quality and service in the industry, in tandem with an overarching desire to do some good in the world, have never wavered. The results are evident, as measured by feedback from customers, other companies in the Medtronic network, and employee feedback.

Between 1998 and 2000, Medtronic's employee base doubled because of acquisitions and expansion. Still, the most recent biennial employee survey, returned by nearly 80% of the workforce, showed consistently high favorable opinions on questions about the company's mission.

Ninety-two percent marked a favorable response to the statement, "The work I do supports the Medtronic mission," and 93% agreed they "have a clear understanding" of the mission. "Medtronic's mission is consistent with my personal values," rang true for 87% of respondents, and 86% said they were proud to tell people they work for Medtronic.

"You can't take that understanding and support for granted," Collins says. "You've got to continue to talk about the mission, to take questions about it, and to challenge it. It's even more valid to do so today in the post-Enron environment with continual corporate scandals."

That type of commitment, Collins says, pays off on the long-term bottom line and makes a company less vulnerable to economic slowdowns. Fiscal year 2003 marked the 18th consecutive year that Medtronic increased earnings and revenues, with about 20% generated by new products. Reflecting the company's focus on innovation, nearly 2/3 of current revenues have come from products introduced in the previous two years.

Because of the company's stellar performance over the long haul, Gene Walden ranked Medtronic shares as the #1 stock to own in his sixth edition of the *Best Stocks to Own in America.* And *Forbes* included Medtronic in its "Platinum 400 List," a recognition of exceptional financials and growth in both sales and earnings.

Less tangible, but no less important, *Fortune* magazine editors have named Medtronic one of "America's Most Admired Companies" seven years in a row and ranked the company first in its industry for six consecutive years. In early 2004 *Fortune* named Medtronic as one of the "100 Best Companies to Work For" for the sixth time in the list's seven-year history.

In addition, *Sales & Marketing Management* has voted Medtronic the "Best Corporate Culture" in the United States, and editors of *Business Ethics* magazine have consistently included the company on its annual list of the nation's "100 Best Corporate Citizens." Medtronic also is on *Forbes*' "A-List," which recognizes the world's 400 best big companies based on sales, profit, return on capital, stock performance, and earning estimates. *BusinessWeek's* annual list of the top 50 best-performing large companies based upon sales and earnings growth, return on equity, and shareholder returns put Medtronic at #21 in 2003.

No doubt those accolades thrill Medtronic leaders and shareholders. But they're not the real reason the company's employees come to work each day with a sense of purpose. Their enthusiasm can be traced back to stories like the one told several years ago at the holiday program by another man whose life had been saved by a Medtronic pacemaker. His son works for the company, not as a scientist or a salesperson, but as a manager unaccustomed to interacting with patients or their doctors.

"One night after he'd been with Medtronic awhile, he called home," his father told the audience. They chatted, then his son quietly said, "Dad, I saved a life today."

For more information on the Medtronic story, go to www.medtronic.com.

13

Southwest Airlines: Flying Direct For Fun And Profits

"If you feel inclined to smoke, please step onto the wing and become a performer in our upcoming movie, *Gone With the Wind*," the flight attendant said with a sly smile. Typifying the Southwest Airlines spirit of fun, her witty safety instructions shortly before take-off grabbed the passengers' attention and kept it. The first airline to inject humor into the usually sleep-inducing announcements, Southwest has been a breath of fresh air from the beginning.

People thought founder and Chairman Herb Kelleher was kidding when he announced his unconventional plans to launch a low-cost, point-to-point airline focused on having fun. When Southwest's first flight took off in June 1971, competitors, industry insiders, and business analysts were among the skeptics who predicted that the maverick businessman's company would be short lived. Few imagined that by the turn of the 21st century, Kelleher's brainchild would have secured its ranking as one of the top four U.S. airlines for domestic travel. Fewer still imagined that Southwest would be the only major airline turning a profit throughout an industry turndown lasting several years.

Outlining his thoughts on a napkin with cofounder Rollin King a few years before starting Southwest, Kelleher defined his mission as providing exceptional customer service with a sense of family warmth, friendliness, individual pride, and most of all, corporate spirit fueled by a large dose of fun. He brought his vision to life by creating a casual, upbeat culture framed by a flattened management structure that facilitates teamwork. From the beginning, managers and employees have worked side by side, doing whatever needed to be done. Kelleher led the way, performing such mundane tasks as loading baggage.

Like other companies that use storytelling as a management tool, Southwest owes part of its success to telling a clear and consistent story about who it is and what it does. Unlike most of the others, Southwest focuses not on stories of employee successes, although such stories are part of the communications mix, but on telling and enacting the *company's* story of management/employee teamwork. Through their actions and a variety of internal media, members of the executive team continually remind employees, "We're in this together, and each of you is critical to our success." Through their collective actions, corporate team members *are* the Southwest story.

One example of the extraordinary teamwork is the way Southwest delivers on its core value of being a low-cost airline, which allows them to offer low fares even for last-minute travel. The airline's operational costs are astoundingly low, largely because its 25-minute flight turnaround maximizes efficiency, and because the airline's trailblazing point-to-point (no-hub) system eliminates costly facility maintenance and complex aircraft routing. But employees also make a significant contribution to cost containment. Flight attendants, for example, help clean the cabins between flights. And pilots, who log more hours than their counterparts at other airlines, often assist baggage handlers. At the urging of management, office employees recycle everything from paper clips to paper scraps, which are used in place of notepads, and employees at every level respond to management's search for ways to cut costs. Flight attendant Rhonda Holley's idea of using plain onboard waste bags instead of logo-imprinted sacks saved the airline $300,000 a year.

Employees' willingness to help with tasks outside their own job responsibilities has resulted in unit labor costs as much as 22% lower than competitors' with similar salary structures. Between 1990 and 1994, when the industry as a whole lost $12 billion, Southwest turned in both operating and net profits, the only airline to do so. And in its 30th anniversary year, Southwest's unorthodox management techniques stood up to unusually intense pressure. The combined turbulence of a major downturn in the U.S. economy, the transition to a new CEO and new President, and the 2001 terrorist attacks did not deter Southwest from its course. The company showed a profit as the rest of the major airlines fell deeper into debt. The bottom line, Southwest President Colleen Barrett explains, is that "part of our working environment means working our butts off."

The hard work is balanced by another key part of the working environment: having fun. Kelleher set the tone from the beginning by deliberately injecting silliness into the workplace. He initiated the practice of throwing frequent employee parties, including costume contests at Halloween, and he's achieved legendary status in the business world with such stunts as dressing like Elvis for an advertising campaign. The management team continues to encourage employees to unleash their senses of humor wherever and whenever they see an opportunity, and in true team spirit, they respond with enthusiasm.

Southwest's remarkable teamwork personifies the Southwest Spirit, a term Kelleher coined to encapsulate the company's core values. "The Southwest Spirit" was the theme of one advertising campaign, but it's far more than a slogan. It's a true reflection of the culture. Joyce C. Rogge, Senior Vice

President—Marketing, explains, "The fun is in the camaraderie, the pulling together. There are no I's but a lot of We's. We certainly can't be lighthearted about airplane maintenance and the responsibilities of our pilots, but as Herb has often been quoted, 'We take the business and the competition seriously; we just don't take ourselves too seriously.'"

Rogge continues, "We couldn't have one of the best safety records and *the* best customer satisfaction rating in the industry if we didn't have a lot of pride in what we do. But that doesn't mean people can't enjoy themselves."

The story of The Southwest Spirit is reinforced at every turn. Beverly Carmichael, Vice President—People, says the company nourishes its spirit in a number of ways. The first step is to hire individuals who share the company's core values, which ensures that new employees will fit into the culture. Then the message that "we're a team" is reinforced in employee orientation sessions and all other corporate training programs. And that message is repeated continuously. It appears on employees' computer screens when they begin work each day, and it's repeated in videos and newsletters sent to employees' homes, messages distributed in corporate mailboxes, and flyers posted in break rooms. A practice that Barrett initiated when she was Executive Vice President—Customer Service has since become part of the culture. Customer letters are collected each month and packets are sent to supervisors' homes. The supervisors select a few stories to tell at their team meetings as examples of what it takes to succeed at Southwest. At the face-to-face staff meetings, managers also share the latest news. "We almost overdo communications," Carmichael explains, "because we always have a third of our employees in the air."

Honoring employees who deliver extraordinary service is another way the airline tells the story of The Southwest Spirit.

Inspired by T. Scott Gross' book, *Positively Outrageous Service,* which features a number of stories about Southwest, the company instituted a monthly Winning Spirit Award. Employees are selected on the basis of customer letters lauding their exceptional level of service. As Gross describes it, outrageous service is giving customers more than they even hope for, making their experience unforgettable and motivating them to return again and again. Southwest followed the creation of the Winning Spirit Award with its own book of outrageous service stories for internal use. "We're collecting new ones all the time," Carmichael says, "because storytelling is a dynamic process."

Southwest ensures that employees know what's expected by treating all 34,000 the same way *they* are expected to treat the customer. And The Southwest Spirit strikes a chord with customers just as it does with employees. The strong corporate spirit is normally evident as soon as passengers arrive at the ticket counter. Employee uniforms, unlike the formal, military-like uniforms of other carriers, are sporty outfits, and gate employees as well as flight attendants seem to be enjoying themselves. When passengers step aboard, they're welcomed with cheerful smiles, and the fun begins as soon as takeoff preparations get underway. Southwest originated the practice of injecting humor into safety procedures, and it's an approach that works well. Longtime airline passengers have heard flight safety instructions so many times that they seldom listen to straightforward directives. But on Southwest flights, they pay attention because they don't want to miss a good joke.

At the end of one flight, for example, as the plane taxied to the gate, the attendant cautioned everyone to remain seated because, "The cockpit crew are better pilots than drivers." On a particularly bumpy flight, another attendant cautioned passengers to remain seated "until Captain Hop-a-Long bounces us to the gate." Attendants on many other airlines have since copied that style.

Some critics try to make the point that, while amusing comments entertain passengers, the remarks aren't professional or reassuring. That argument is easily countered by pointing out the wisdom of entertaining people with information that otherwise would be ignored. Informative safety instructions that also entertain are prime examples of effective communications. Like stories, they capture attention, get the point across, and make the message memorable.

Even Southwest's lack of full meal service, a cost-control policy that contributes to keeping fares low, helps to reinforce the spirit of fun. Since Southwest serves only drinks and snacks, passengers on long flights need to bring aboard their own meals, and the practice creates a casual, picnic-like atmosphere.

For Southwest employees, the motivation for enjoying their work goes beyond awards and stories of individuals who deliver outrageous service. A major reason for their enthusiasm and sense of fun is the company's long-standing compensation policies, which substantiate the teamwork message. Just a few years after the company's launch, Southwest created the industry's first profit-sharing plan, and in 1984 the company added a stock-purchase plan to the employee benefits package. Stock options followed a few years after that, and a period of soaring stock prices subsequently turned many employees into millionaires. Instead of retiring, though, most continued working. The Southwest Spirit had created a dedicated and loyal workforce, and employees have demonstrated their dedication and loyalty in other remarkable ways.

During one downturn in the U.S. economy that threatened the necessity for layoffs, employees removed any doubt about the spirit of camaraderie. Instead of resigning themselves to losing members of the Southwest "family," many volunteered to take reductions in hours and pay in the short term so everyone would continue receiving a steady paycheck. Then they worked harder to ensure that outrageous service would continue. Some even worked extra hours without pay, and pilots agreed to stock options instead of pay increases. Echoing Barrett in saying that the airline's work ethic is critical to its success, CEO James Parker adds, "Our cost advantage is not based on low wages. We pay very competitive wages. Our advantage is based on our employees' hard work."

Even a loyal team that enjoys its work gets weary, however, and Southwest has not been without labor problems. A prolonged recession following the turn of the 21st century took a toll on management/employee relations and somewhat dampened The Southwest Spirit. At one point, an employee expressed a seldom-heard complaint to a news reporter, grumbling that employees were working at their peak and had no more to give. Negotiations with labor unions dragged on, causing some business analysts to question whether Southwest had become too big to maintain the unique practices that had created and nurtured the culture. Despite the ups and downs, however, the often-repeated story of low cost and high cheer continued to drive operations.

Kelleher believes the strength of the camaraderie is largely a result of giving employees what they need from their work. In an interview with AOL, Kelleher said that employee ownership of the company is only one motivating factor. "I think people are looking for psychic satisfaction in what they do—particularly today," he said, "and we try to remain cognizant of that."

Carmichael adds, "We work constantly to ensure that employees know how our family spirit looks and feels, and the caring family attitude has grown over the years. We have a low turnover rate, and...[because] people stay with us a long time, the culture becomes embedded in them."

By any measure, Southwest's maverick founder and chairman has proved his formula for running a profitable airline. The ability to deliver low-cost, point-to-point service with a large dose of fun and a plethora of stories has spawned imitators and made believers of early skeptics. Constant nurturing of The Southwest Spirit has kept the dedicated team on board. And clear, continuous storytelling remains a key factor in transforming unorthodox ideas into impressive results.

For more on the Southwest Airlines story, go to www.swair.com.

14

The Container Store:
Have You Heard The One About Tales That Boost The Bottom Line?

Picture the proverbial man lost in the desert, hauling himself across miles of sand dunes, desperate for just one sip of water. Finally he comes to an oasis. Summoning a last spurt of energy, he drags himself up to it and finds a run-of-the-mill retail store. As a salesperson hands him a drink of water, the man cries, "I'm saved!"

Now imagine the same situation, but this time the man crawls up to The Container Store (TCS) and has a very different experience. A TCS employee would describe it like this: "Sure, we would give him water. Then we would ask, 'How about some food? And I see you have a wedding ring on. Can we contact your family and let them know you're here? And how would you like some shade?'"

This man-in-the-desert metaphor reminds employees of one of the store founders' six guiding principles: give customers a one-of-a-kind shopping experience. When employees hear the story, they know it's time to rededicate themselves to solving everything from the most minute storage problems to the most intimidating organizational challenges. The story keeps the founders' do-unto-others vision in sharp focus: create the best retail store in the United States, offer customers the best products available, provide impeccable customer service with fair pricing, and treat customers and employees alike with respect and integrity.

The belief is that TCS' adaptation of the Golden Rule makes customers feel special, and in turn, employees feel like helpful public servants rather than pushy sales clerks. TCS salespeople don't say to customers, "I just did something nice for you." They just do it.

"Filling the other guy's basket to the brim" is another core principle, a concept borrowed from Andrew Carnegie. Ironically, this approach is so unique that it's usually about a year before customers in a new market realize that clerks are so nice because they just want to help, says Barbara Anderson, official keeper of the culture. "Customers simply don't expect wonderful treatment!"

The rest of TCS' Foundation Principles are:

- One great person equals three good (productive) people, so hire only great people.
- Intuition is essential in our business, but it doesn't come to an unprepared mind. Prepare people through training.
- Offer the best selection anywhere, the best service anywhere, and the best or equal-to-best pricing in our markets.
- Create and maintain an air of excitement in every store.

Kip Tindell, President and CEO of The Container Store, cites filling-the-other-guy's-basket as just one of many analogies used over the years to remind employees of the company's founding principles. Those guidelines have helped the founders, Tindell and Chairman Garret Boone, build one of the top retail companies in the U.S.

Product value also is important at The Container Store, although higher price points may run counter to a typical retailers' definition of "value." AT TCS, items may cost 20%

more than their competitors', but the founders believe that their products function 100% better, look 150% better, and last 50% longer. That's a priceless lesson Tindell and Boone learned early on from Neiman Marcus Chairman Emeritus Stanley Marcus.

"If today's specialty retailers want to delight, inspire and win loyal customers for life, they must provide the complete solution to customers' problems," Tindell says. The company's style—often copied, seldom duplicated—revolves around providing solutions to help customers save space and, ultimately, time. Cost isn't the overriding factor. Value is.

Barbara Anderson points out that the company's founders communicated these ideas through stories right from the start, and anecdotes resonate even better now than in 1978, when the first store opened in Dallas. Especially after the tragic events of September 11, 2001, she notes, America has been "turning to heroic stories to find stability...to find our roots."

Tindell demonstrated his skill in creating word pictures as a motivational tool when he wrote an article for Texas A&M's publication, *The Retail Issues Letter*. "Think about some of your favorite things, such as a cherished baseball mitt," he wrote. "Every time you see it or slip it on your hand, it evokes that timeless memory of the catch you made in the most important game of the season.

"Or what about that one dish only Mom could cook? You don't know how much money I would pay to have my grandmother's rice and gravy again...that comforting feeling when you eat it...passed down from generation to generation.

"Or your favorite pair of pajamas, the ones you put on during a rainy evening at home. They're so cozy and make you feel warm and secure. They just, well, make you happy.

"At The Container Store," he continues, "we try to evoke those same emotions, those same memories, those same connections, with our products."

Tindell promises customers they'll notice an "air of excitement" before they take more than three steps inside the front door. Every operational decision the founders make—generating fun included—contributes to creating an exciting atmosphere.

Despite the cyclical nature of retailing, nothing in Tindell and Boone's core strategy has changed since they started the company more than 25 years ago. The remarkable power of their basic idea "captures a fundamental, enduring need of human beings to do something with possessions they're not currently holding in their hands—to not only put them away, but put them away in their proper places," Tindell told Leonard L. Berry, author of the groundbreaking book, *Discovering the Soul of Service.* The book is filled with case studies from service-centric companies that have been able to sustain long-term success.

So what does The Container Store actually sell? "The hard stuff," Tindell answers, products that need explanation to show their multifunctional uses. And that reminds him of another story.

One morning it was discovered that a merchandise-filled truck parked overnight outside the Dallas distribution center was missing. The long-haul rig was eventually found several miles away, its lock broken and its back door pried open. Thieves had rifled through seven or eight cartons of foam—the kind you cut with scissors to fit any size drawer—but left the rest of the boxes untouched in frustration. As Tindall explains, not only does TCS offer hard-to-sell products, they also sell products people won't even steal! He chuckles at the thought.

Other articles that thieves might not understand well enough to steal include elfa®, a modular wire drawer and shelving system, and wire leaf burners turned into toy barrels. Then, of course, there's the ubiquitous milk crate. In the fertile minds of TCS' sales staff and customers, it's no longer a milk crate; it's a file container, bedside table, storage unit, and even a sturdy stepstool for washing the top of an SUV. Its uses are limited only by the creativity of the buyer's imagination, which is readily sparked by floor displays throughout the spacious stores, which average 25,000 square feet.

Managers expect their sales teams to literally think outside the box. This philosophy is reinforced by putting the same product in many different sections of the store—Closet, Kitchen, Office, and Laundry, for example—to prevent it from being pigeonholed by preconceptions. This finding-new-uses-for-old-items way of thinking also shows up on the cover of a company catalog. One issue featured a silver-handled, white plastic shower tote used 14 different ways—from dog carrier to champagne bucket to lamp.

Then there's the elfa white-wire component shelving and drawer system, The Container Store's best-selling product. Because most customers need help configuring a customized storage system that fits their space, it's a perfect product for a store that provides impeccable service. Selling the systems requires time, both to explain the options and to build the customer's trust. But, CEO Tindell says, the result can change customers' lives forever, particularly when TCS succeeds in designing "a closet that makes them do a little dance every time they open the door."

The Container Store carries about 10,000 more products that are equally hard to sell—so hard that most retailers don't want to touch them. According to Tindell, though, "With a little story, a little interaction, all these products can be transformed into lifesavers."

Oral storytelling also is used to teach the company's Foundation Principles. Policy manuals don't exist because "we don't have time to read around here," Barbara Anderson laughs. Instead, each employee is expected to know and practice the principles, and also to teach them to others, primarily through story. One of a manager's main responsibilites is to reinforce the principles by sharing sales success stories. Managers are both mentors and role models, and even the founders can be seen working the floor, dusting shelves, and helping customers.

"We tell managers and trainers, 'Here are the points you should cover,'" Anderson explains, "but we don't write them down in complete sentences. That way, people have to use their own personal style, not ours."

When The Container Store last surveyed employees, the leadership team discovered about 85% could repeat the company's Foundation Principles—not by rote, of course, but in their own words. "We're committed to our staff *living* these values, not just repeating them," Anderson adds, "and stories are the most effective management tool we've found to help them understand what our values really mean.

"Employees also make up the rules, corporate doesn't. Initially, some new-hires find it scary to have to make their own decisions. We're so different that our employees call other companies 'the other world.' Ours is an atmosphere not easy to create and not easy to sustain, but crucial to our success."

While Anderson is the keeper of the culture, the job of keeping it alive belongs to everybody. "We expect employees to come up with anecdotes about *their* store and *their* staff," she says. The most fertile ground for these stories? Daily cheerleading sessions. Before opening for business each morning, and again after closing, the team in each store huddles to tell stories of what worked and what didn't.

The manager collects the best tales and sends them to headquarters for sharing:

- In daily "celebration" voice-mailbox messages
- In the company newsletter
- During the first week of training when new-hires find out what makes The Container Store tick
- In company-wide staff meetings
- When department heads celebrate an employee's first-year anniversary

Increasing sales is, of course, a critical objective of these twice-daily huddles. Depending on sales numbers for key items, the focus of the stories shifts from product to product, and momentum builds for each in turn. Managers call this "the swing of the pendulum," and they are clear about harnessing its power to positively impact the bottom line. In one case, for example, when sales of the elfa storage systems began to slip, managers focused on collecting stories describing successful approaches to selling the systems. The bottom-line result: sales and profits swung back up.

As demonstrated by TCS's performance, the storytelling approach to management consistently works. A privately held, national company with 30 stores in 15 markets and growing, The Container Store also runs a thriving national mail-order service and an online store. Retail sales have enjoyed healthy increases each year, according to the company's Web site. While TCS does not make its financial statements public, total sales for 2004 are estimated at more than $370 million. And the strong, people-oriented culture that Tindell and Boone have created for their 2,500+ employees has led to top rankings on *Fortune* magazine's list of the "100 Best Companies to Work For" five years in a row. TCS captured the top spot in

2000 and 2001, #2 in 2002 and 2003 and #3 in 2004. According to *Fortune*, the retailer's employees remain "enthusiastic about good pay, great benefits and respect." Another tribute to the company's successful formula was the Retail Innovator's Award from the National Retail Federation in 1999.

Anecdotes also lie at the heart of the company's 10-year-service dinners. Honorees tell what the company has meant to them, and their managers reciprocate with stories about the employees' successes. In addition, managers write thank-you notes to recognize extraordinary efforts by staff members. Many of these notes hang framed in recipients' offices. The founders also get into the act by writing notes of appreciation to every employee mentioned in a customer commendation letter.

Tindell believes leadership and communication are one and the same. That's why he and his partner share nearly every detail of the business with employees, from daily sales numbers to expansion plans. "Every single employee gets the previous day's sales results, and we make the daily sales goals clear" before the workday starts.

"Think about a football game. All players must know the score of the game and the team objective if they're going to contribute. Imagine the two-minute warning sounding. You're driving down the field, determined to pull out a last-minute, come-from-behind victory...the ultimate team adventure...and you have two guys sitting on the bench who don't even know the score. What good are they?"

Financial data does occasionally fall into the wrong hands, but Tindell and Boone have not wavered on their decision to share "inside" information. They believe open communication empowers employees, strengthens their development, enhances their contributions, and reinforces their loyalty. In the founders' view, these benefits far outweigh the risks.

Self-described "wild-eyed fanatics" when it comes to hiring great people, The Container Store's managers are prepared to hold out for as long as it takes to find the person whose ideals and ethics match the corporate culture. Recruitment, however, is not difficult. Instead of placing help-wanted ads, the company prefers to pay its own employees to find new talent. Nearly 40% percent of new-hires are recruited by current staff. In some stores, it's 90%, a figure that exemplifies the Foundation Principle of "One great person equals three good people." After great people are hired, they're given the gift of another of the founding principles: an obsession for learning. Every new full-time employee gets 241 hours of training the first year. The retail-industry average? Seven hours.

Training starts with 50 hours of instruction the first week(this takes place in the back room and on the sales floor). Then, and every year thereafter, both new and current employees spend dozens of hours with Sales Trainers. This training is sometimes formalized with a small group or can also be "off the cuff." The trainers are not only key salespeople in the stores, but also responsible for big-picture knowledge, such as sales techniques, down to the tiniest details, such as material used in product manufacturing, or how the item will work in a quirky situation or space. Trainers often use storytelling to ensure that lessons stick.

The company's strong commitment to continuing education is inspired by a well-known story about how Albert Einstein made his greatest discovery. According to legend, he was sitting in a train car waiting for departure when a train on the adjacent track pulled out. Einstein noticed that he had the sensation of his own train moving, even though it wasn't. The resulting flash of intuition, based on a lifetime of studying physics and math, led Einstein to the Theory of Relativity. One man's commitment to ongoing study changed the way humankind perceives the world.

"The best selection anywhere, plus best service anywhere, plus best-or-equal-to-best pricing in the market area" is another Foundation Principle contributing to The Container Store's success. Combined with a strategy of developing new and exclusive products in partnership with manufacturers, this principle has led to impressive sales numbers. Each of TCS' retail outlets draws nearly 1,000 customers through the doors every day, comparable to the streams of traffic in grocery stores, and sales-per-square-foot have been several times the industry average.

To be called "Gumby-like" is the highest compliment for any TCS employee. The cartoon character epitomizes the flexibility that the company expects its people to practice. That's why likenesses of Gumby can be seen on the sales floor, in offices, on shelves, and in many other places around the company. Even one of the conference rooms at the Dallas headquarters—the room easily reconfigured for large meetings or small—bears Gumby's name.

Compliments and recognition can indeed motivate, and that's why so many companies claim that employees are their most important asset. Few companies, however, also demonstrate their sincerity with salaries that are 50-100% above retail industry average with no cap. For more than 25 years, The Container Store has allocated 18% of its revenues for salaries and wages.

Commissions are not part of the compensation package; the founders believe that commissions promote competition among employees rather than teamwork. "Sometimes it's even hard to find out who the manager is," Anderson laughs, recalling a recurring story. "If a customer asks for the manager, every salesperson will say, 'Here I am. What can I do for you?' No seniority. No politics. Individuals have the freedom to make the type of decisions usually reserved for top managers in most other stores."

Hiring great people and paying them well requires determination, vision, and "more bravery" than just about anything else the company leaders do, Tindell acknowledges. That's especially true when faced with the challenge of a slowdown in the business economy in 2001, which led to a decrease in customer demand. Higher-than-average pay, though, is part of the commitment to maintaining a great environment that enables people to grow. And that commitment pays off. In the face of a weak economy, it can mean the difference between merely surviving on sluggish sales and outdistancing competitors with a mounting bottom line.

Generosity with information and monetary rewards also forge bonds of loyalty and longevity. The Container Store's employee turnover rate of less than 20% on average and around 8% for full-time employees is a tiny blip on the radar screen compared with the 150% industry average. Tindell explains it this way: "A funny thing happens when you take the time to educate employees, pay them well, and treat them as equals. You end up with extremely motivated and enthusiastic people. That reminds me. Have you heard the one about how we came up with the billboard, 'We Can Help You Get At Least One Car In Your Two-Car Garage'?"

Like its myriad of products, TCS' collection of stories is diverse. There are tales about its Foundation Principles, employee successes, customer feedback, unusual retailing experiences, and solving nearly any storage dilemma. Have you heard the one about closets too jammed to open, kitchen cupboards too full to find what you need, or different ways to use a waste basket?

For more information on The Container Store story, go to www.thecontainerstore.com.

15

REI:

Attaining The Peak Of Authenticity

Mountain climbers often plant their nation's flag at the summit to commemorate a successful expedition. In their quest for quality climbing gear, Lloyd and Mary Anderson went directly to the best Austrian sources and unintentionally planted the seeds of a successful nationwide retailer.

"It all started with an ice axe," says Sally Jewell, Executive Vice President and COO of the now-renowned Recreational Equipment, Inc. (REI), in her straightforward fashion that befits the cooperative's style. "We tell the story on our Web site, and when Dennis [Madsen, REI's President and CEO] and I address employee groups, we sometimes tell the story to remind everyone of our roots. So most of our employees know the story of Lloyd and Mary Anderson, members #1 and #2, who led a group of friends in forming this co-op in 1938. They did it to access good European climbing gear because the suppliers didn't have an interest in shipping onesies and twosies."

The quest for high quality and authenticity helped REI quickly establish a reputation throughout the climbing world as a premier supplier of gear, and a low membership number became a source of pride for climbers and other outdoor enthusiasts. The co-op's reputation was greatly enhanced by the early involvement of people such as Jim Whittaker, who in 1963 became the first American to reach the top of Mt. Everest and later served as President and CEO of REI. Gradually the co-op expanded the product mix in response to customer demand and has for many years carried equipment for backpacking, skiing, and other popular outdoor activities. The product list eventually grew to include all "muscle-powered activities," such as kayaking, snowboarding, and in recent years, travel. Now the largest consumer co-operative in the U.S., and likely in the world, REI's reach extends to more than 40 countries, and active membership totals more than two million. The list of options for how those members and other customers can make purchases also has expanded. In addition to nearly 70 retail stores in 24 states and plans for more, REI's integrated sales system includes telephone, direct mail, catalog, and Web-based transactions. Customers can even place Internet orders at in-store kiosks on the sales floor.

Although the climbing gear and the range of equipment look much different today from the goods offered in 1938, the guiding principles of the consumer co-op have not changed. The REI story is still about love of the outdoors, and authenticity is still the uppermost core value. The Seattle flagship store and other relatively new facilities tell the co-op's story through the mountain-lodge building design, natural materials, and features such as a practice rock-climbing wall and indoor trails with different surfaces for testing footwear. "Authenticity, meaning true to the outdoors, that's what REI is all about," Jewell says. "When this was a smaller company, people usually knew that they were joining a co-op, that they technically owned the company, and that they would receive a dividend based on their purchases at the end of the year. The story was pretty clear to everyone. The challenge as REI continues to grow is this: How do we maintain a level of understanding among our employees and our more traditional customers that we are changing to meet customers' demands but that we also are remaining authentic and true to the outdoors and our roots?"

Following its first bottom-line loss and a number of changes in management personnel and priorities in 2000, the leadership team spent 18 months in intensive self-examination when Madsen and Jewell were named to their current positions. They set out to rethink the REI story and update it appropriately. As Jewell describes the process, "Adversity brings opportunity and, as a company, we understood the need to articulate our unchanging values. Values are old friends that help you cope with all the changes that surround all of us. It also was important to identify what was true of our story in 1938 that is still true today and will remain true in 2038." To find out, the leaders gathered input from the Board of Directors and 174 people then on REI's management team. The goal of the project was to clearly articulate the co-op's core purpose.

Inspired by James C. Collins' and Jerry Porras' book, *Built to Last*, REI's former Vice President of Public Affairs, Kathleen Beamer, developed a customized questionnaire for participants. Each was instructed to write down answers to a series of questions, beginning with *What does REI do?* and including such probing queries as *What would be lost if REI ceased to exist?* To get to REI's core purpose, the survey followed the answer to each question with *Why is that important?*

A section of one completed questionnaire went like this: *What does REI do?* "Provides quality and dependable equipment for entertainment outdoors and creates a reputable workplace for many." *Why is that important?* "People need to embrace, enjoy, and respect the outdoors and keep a balance in this fast-paced, stressful world." *Why is that important?* "Being good people and good parents is better for the community. We all need to live together and work together, and we need to make the world in which we live a better place for future generations."

After each of the 174 participants' questionnaires was carefully reviewed, a clear direction for a simply-expressed purpose statement emerged. The finished document tells of the co-op's mission to educate and outfit its customers for a lifetime of outdoor adventure."

This purpose statement has been shared throughout the company, along with reinforcement of REI's core values:

- Authenticity—true to the outdoors
- Quality—products and services you can trust
- Service—pride in supporting our customers, communities, and colleagues
- Respect—people are valued and recognized for their accomplishments (employees and everyone who walks through the door)
- Honesty—rock-solid integrity in all actions
- Balance—work smart, have fun

"What's neat about the process outlined in *Built to Last*," Jewell says, "is that it leads you to the expressions of authenticity we were searching for. As a co-op, we go beyond just selling products and making a profit to sustain ourselves and grow. We have a higher calling, which is becoming stewards for the environment." To fulfill that role, the company sets aside a portion of its profits each year for support of conservation and recreation, with an annual commitment of just under $2 million.

In an extraordinary demonstration of walking the talk, both literally and figuratively, Madsen and the other members of the leadership team enact the core values—particularly respect for employees—by spreading the REI story *in person*. The practice began in 2001, when Madsen and crew visited every single store between November and December. They gave each employee a wallet card mounted inside a printed thank-you note developed for the occasion. The card acknowledged employees for their trust and constant dedication to serving customers as the management team tackled the challenges of the previous year.

The every-store visit has since become an annual event, with every member of the leadership team taking part. They assure employees of REI's full commitment to its mission and discuss the year ahead. They also share an updated longer-term view into the future and remind the staff how they can best serve the co-op's members. As they present each staff member with a specially-designed gift to thank them for their efforts, leaders also invite feedback from all of the co-op's 6,000+ employees.

Although the national tour of all stores is limited to a once-a-year event, interaction between REI's management team and employees is the norm. Madsen and Jewell conduct quarterly meetings for all employees at corporate headquarters and at the distribution center to provide a forum for direct conversation, and all managers take part in strategic planning at the annual leadership conference, which includes time for outdoor group activities. To enhance direct communication at all levels, the number of stores that district managers oversee dropped from 20 to around 10, which allows them to spend more time on individual coaching and gives them more opportunities to share best practices. All the managers have a toolkit of success stories they share about REI employees, usually people in their own district, and the heroes of the success stories are rewarded with a gift certificate as well as public recognition in the store. Employees also have an opportunity for one-on-one conversations with the CEO through the co-op's intranet. Through the "Ask Dennis" forum, any employee can ask Madsen a work-related question. Over 3,200 entries have been logged since the July 2001 launch.

To ensure that everyone remains close to the core business, to one another, and to customers' wants and needs, every exempt employee is required to work on the sales floor once per quarter. For some members of the leadership team, including Madsen, the retail floor is familiar territory. He started with REI part time in 1966, when he was just 17 and the co-op had just one store in Seattle with 33 employees. In his first position, Madsen stocked shelves. After finishing college, he signed on full time and began working his way up, witnessing a number of major changes along the way. He remembers the co-op's first expansion, when REI built its second store in Berkeley, California, in 1975. Even though 10,000 members were waiting for a bricks-and-mortar presence, a cautious management team saw it as a daring move. Years later, as Executive Vice President and COO, Madsen envisioned the need and led the drive to integrate sales into one multi-channel system to give customers a consistent shopping experience. As a result, REI.com has become the Internet's biggest outdoor retailer, and a 2002 Forrester Research report named the co-op one of the best multi-channel retail companies in the country, citing "the customer experience" as one of REI's strengths.

Extending the definition of customer service even further, the co-op more recently ventured into the travel business. REI Adventures, a full-service adventure travel company that began 17 years ago as a phone- and catalog-based operation, leads all types of expeditions—from the Arctic to the Galapagos Islands. Trips are planned around activities—from mountain climbing to discovery cruising and kayaking—and level of fitness required, ranging from easy to strenuous. The co-op's foray into the travel business includes clothing, and

Jewell acknowledges that some employees have expressed concern that this latest extension of the REI brand represents a move away from the core business. "They're fearful that we'll be distracted by the allure of higher margins on clothing and lose sight of our core purpose to be a respected, true hard goods outdoor retailer. But our customers have created a demand for easy-care garments that travel well. As we baby-boomers age, many of us aren't climbing mountains anymore. But when we visit different parts of the world, we want quick-drying, attractive fabrics with a nice drape that will provide appropriate cover for attending church in Italy or visiting Afghanistan. REI is an expert on cultural differences, and we know, for example, that in many parts of the world, sandals are not allowed. Providing appropriate travel garments is, in our view, being true to our story as a provider of high-quality, authentic goods for outdoor pursuits."

Outdoors enthusiasts like many other employees, Jewell and Madsen both list mountain climbing among their favorite activities, and they've changed the focus of the employee newsletter to a more casual approach that features active employees at work and play. One issue shows Product Developer Bill Hartlieb climbing Black Peak in Washington state with other REI employees to test prototype gear. Telling the story of their strenuous ascent, it describes the punishment that they inflicted on the gear. A sidebar story relates how important it is for product development to get employee feedback from their personal use of REI equipment.

REI also ensures that it keeps its commitment to the local communities near its stores by encouraging and supporting employee involvement in outdoor events. Madsen says, "We're privileged to be able to give something back to the outdoors, and to help those who don't have easy access to enjoy the muscle-powered activities we love." Employees volunteer to help at events such as bike races and marathons, and helping customers evaluate which equipment is right for them is also seen as a community service. This is especially true when a customer is beginning a new sport, or when parents are looking for the appropriate gear for their children. "There are no commissions," Jewell points out. "Our people are here for the right reason, and they do the right thing."

REI's focus on staying true to its stated purpose, maintaining an authentic corporate culture, and telling its story clearly has produced remarkable results with employees and with customers. The co-op has been recognized seven years in a row as one of *Fortune* magazine's "100 Best Companies to Work For." And it's one of only nine organizations that have been on every one of the magazine's annual lists and in both book versions.

Having worked with all four of the company's previous CEOs, including founder Lloyd Anderson, Dennis Madsen appreciates the organization's heritage and his role as the official keeper of the culture. He's also excited about shaping REI's story for the future. Leading the company from its first and only year of losses in 2000 to record profits and sales of well over $805 million in 2003, Madsen sees a future of continual expansion and enhanced customer service. "The outdoors and outdoor lifestyle are still very near and dear to many people's hearts in this country," he says.

Among REI's plans are more new stores, renovated stores, and a stronger emphasis on designing and selling its own branded gear and outerwear. "We will continue to look for new ways to serve our members' needs, just as our founders did," Madsen says. "And we will continue to tell the story of Lloyd and Mary Anderson.

It still resonates with our employees more than 60 years later because it's about real people whose commitment to quality and authenticity still drive our organization."

For more information on the REI story, go to www.rei.com.

16

Not For Corporations Only

The corporate stories in this collection illustrate the numerous purposes for which a storytelling system can be put to work:

- Convey information/share knowledge (all the companies featured)
- Clarify and underscore the mission (3M)
- Personify the mission (Medtronic)
- Underscore the values (Costco)
- Sell a product/service and/or persuade others to a point of view (Fox's Gem Shop)
- Inspire dedication to the mission (Nike, Southwest Airlines)
- Establish and solidify teams (The Container Store, WRQ)
- Reach consensus (REI)
- Cope with emotions in a crisis (Northwestern Mutual)
- Nurture and enhance a corporate culture (Armstrong International)
- Honor tradition (Eastman Kodak)
- Celebrate successes (Mary Kay, Inc.)
- Recognize individual achievement (FedEx)
- Build personal connections between and among management and staff (K/P Corporation)

These applications of storytelling are equally effective in other types of organizations, the most notable being social service agencies, medical institutions, churches, educational institutions, international communities, and government agencies.

Social service agencies have long understood the importance of storytelling, and they have proved the power of personal stories in garnering support for a cause or campaign. Brief stories of a family's or a child's plight, often accompanied by photos, tug at our hearts and loosen our purse strings. Who can resist the plea to help when you hear a compelling story of someone in need? Even challenges that seemed overwhelming are small by comparison. Some corporations, particularly those in the medical equipment industries like Medtronic, have successfully adapted this personal, heart-tugging approach by featuring stories in their annual reports and employee publications that describe how their devices have saved lives. In its annual report of giving, Microsoft Community Affairs tells how the company's and employees' donations of cash, software, and volunteer efforts have dramatically brightened the future for one or two of the hundreds of people helped by each of their major corporate giving initiatives. In the telling, corporate giving comes alive!

Storytelling is being successfully used in many other types of organizations as well. Increasing numbers of medical institutions and healthcare professionals are recognizing the healing attributes of storytelling. Consultants James D. Henry and Linda G. Henry, who have written three books of healthcare stories in just four years, say that relationship-centered care is a rapidly growing movement. "Relationship-centered care is about listening to one another and holding one's story as sacred," James Henry explains. "The honored physician in this context is the one who starts his/her appointment with you by asking what's going on in your life, or who says, 'Tell me your story.' Listening to the patient's story is part of the healing process and contributes to the necessary balance of physical, mental, and spiritual health. The more patients tell their stories, the more healing occurs."

In their first book, *Reclaiming Soul in Health Care: Practical Strategies for Revitalizing Providers of Care*, the Henrys discuss the importance of reclaiming and enhancing soul in the helping professions. Defining "soul" in the workplace as taking time to meaningfully connect to other people by listening, they address the relationship between soul and a profitable organization. In *The Soul of the Physician: Doctors Speaking about Passion, Resilience, and Hope*, they document the stories of 33 physicians who were invited to relate their personal struggles and triumphs and to discuss their sense of isolation. Published by the American Medical Association, the physicians' story collection is followed by *The Soul of the Caring Nurse: Stories and Resources for Revitalizing Professional Passion*, published by the American Nurses Association in 2004.

Clerics have long understood the power of stories to deliver a message. Following Jesus' example, preachers often intersperse their sermon points with personal stories from their lives or others' as a means of connecting with each person in the congregation. And, similar to the corporate practices described in this book, many church leaders use stories in administrative communications. Leaders of Menlo Park Presbyterian Church, serving a congregation of 6,000 in Menlo Park, California, have been using stories as a management tool and as an element of their worship services for a number of years.

The practice of storytelling at Menlo Park started in earnest with Walt Gerber, who served as senior pastor for 28 years until his retirement in 2002. "Walt's personal style was to tell us what he's learned in life, not what he knows," says Doug Lawrence, Menlo Park's Minister of Worship. "We're all skeptical when others tell us what they know, but if they tell you what they've learned, you have to let them own that. You can't critique someone else's experiences, and that leaves you open to hearing their message." Noting that people often remember stories for years, Lawrence says Gerber preached a Christmas Eve sermon several different times that included a story about birds. "People loved that story so much, we still have some who come to church on Christmas Eve just to hear about the birds again."

The single most effective application of stories at Menlo Park is during worship services, which include a personal testimony nearly every week. During that segment, a member of the congregation recounts a dramatic life change that followed a decision to make a commitment to God. In some cases, the person relates how a church ministry program helped him or her through an overwhelming personal struggle; in other cases, someone shares a dramatic life turn that followed a major financial commitment to the church. "We call it 'expressing our gratitude,'" Lawrence says. "You hear how a person's life was changed, you appreciate the person's willingness to be vulnerable, and you learn how you too can get involved; each story, in effect, endorses all our programs.

"We also find that storytelling is effective with children and teenagers, as well as with the staff. At weekly staff meetings, the question is asked, 'Did you catch anyone doing something right this week?' We assume people have been good to others all week, but noticing someone being especially helpful when they didn't know you were looking really makes the point about the type of behavior we expect in a Christian community. We share those stories all the time."

Lawrence observes that stories are critical in contemporary communications because "we live in a different world...an age when facts are not enough. Knowledge hasn't fixed anything. Churches need to realize that if we're not touched emotionally, we're not going to assimilate the information. My job as worship facilitator is not to educate people; it's to help them get the Gospel message and be transformed by it."

In addition to Harvard Business School's use of case studies, educational institutions are awakening to the value of storytelling in leadership training as well as the more common practice of relating personal experiences for marketing and community relations. Seattle Pacific University is among the schools that inform prospective students, donors, and members of the business community of its nationally recognized programs by telling the stories of students in diverse areas of study. Offering courses in storytelling for leaders is a growing practice. DePaul University's School for New Learning periodically offers a class that includes a component on storytelling in business, and the Mendoza College of Business Executive Integral Leadership program at the University of Notre Dame offered a related session for the first time in August 2003. It was focused on presentation skills, and Paul Slaggert, Director of Non-degree Programs, says participants highly valued that segment of the curriculum.

International community-building often employs stories to help people from different cultures gain understanding and establish bonds. One of the most well-known case studies among organizational development professionals and business storytelling practitioners is about the World Bank. One of the reasons it's so memorable is Steve Denning, who recommended and then launched a successful storytelling initiative at the United Nations agency. Author of *The Springboard: How Storytelling Ignites Action in Knowledge-Era Organizations*, Denning is a proponent of storytelling to effect change, which in his view is the highest value of storytelling. This is an especially timely topic, he says, in this period of "wrenching change the world is going through. Computerization has turned everything upside down and inside down, and the way the human race has always dealt with complexity and change has been through stories. The measure of its effectiveness is, 'Are you getting the actions you intended to get? If you're trying to introduce change, do you see that change happening?'"

At the World Bank, the answer was a resounding "Yes!" During the 1996 annual meeting, the agency's President, James D. Wolfensohn, announced that the World Bank needed to invest in a worldwide knowledge-sharing system, one that would enable any of its 10,000 staff members at any location to gather development information and expertise and share it with the agency's clients. "Springboard" stories were to be the conduit for sharing this knowledge. The idea caught on and spread like wildfire, an anomaly in an agency of 184 member countries that inherently embraces change very slowly. By the year 2000, knowledge management was a budgeted part of the operation and had been integrated into the mission statement. It also had been adopted as part of the strategic plan, and implemented by well over 100 World Bank-assisted communities around the globe. In just four years, the agency had become a leading knowledge management practitioner, with Denning serving as program director.

Now a consultant and thought leader in the organizational storytelling community, Denning says that, simply stated, storytelling is a way of talking persuasively, intelligently, and interestingly—an essential skill for CEOs and other leaders. "That's why business publications such as *The Wall Street Journal*, *Harvard Business Review*, *American Economic Review*, and *CIO* are writing about storytelling. An article in *American Economic Review* presented findings that 28% of business activities is spent on persuasion. Assuming that storytelling represents at least half that, storytelling represents $1.4 trillion of our nation's GNP. Organizations that want to get things done, and those that realize they need to change traditional ways of doing things, need to pay attention to the impact of stories. Again, the measure is: Are you getting the results you intended to get?"

One governmental organization that has discovered the value of storytelling is NASA, which uses the tool for training and knowledge management. The practice began after the agency had been contracting for several years with EduTech Ltd., a technology consulting and training firm. Mildred Lockhart-Boyd, PhD, the firm's President, explains that stories had been part of its training programs for NASA, but had not been a central part of the firm's services until several NASA managers expressed interest in leveraging the power of stories for employee communications. After considering a number of possibilities, EduTech began producing an electronic employee magazine for NASA that features stories of successful team projects. It wasn't long before the agency's employees asked for a print version so they could carry it with them when they traveled.

"Everyone has stories, and everyone loves stories," Dr. Boyd says, "as evidenced by the amazing growth in the magazine's circulation. When we started, we had 200 subscribers; now we have 8,000!

"But the real test of effectiveness is measurement of results. We evaluate the impact of the stories in a number of ways. The number of people asking to be added to the mailing list, the number of requests for reprints, and the cost savings of shared knowledge are a few examples. The most important metric is the impact of dollars saved. In one case, a project manager calculated that a problem-solving technique borrowed from another team helped him save half a million dollars in man hours. We're always looking for ways to assess the human capital impact of the stories we tell.

"Stories definitely save both money and time, and they generate fresh ideas," Dr. Boyd says. "In fact, the use of stories for knowledge sharing has been so effective at NASA, we started using them in similar ways to help our own project teams. We also use stories to tell new employees the history of our firm so they can get a sense of our culture and get to know us more quickly. Our history helps them understand where we've been and where we're going, and, of course, people enjoy seeing their own stories in print. In a number of different ways, storytelling has been of great value to us."

17

Without Stories, What Have You Got?

Storytelling has been the glue connecting people with their communities and with one another throughout human history. In ancient cultures, and even in many modern tribes, the oral tradition was the vehicle for passing tribal practices and history down through the generations. The designated tribal storyteller was responsible for ensuring that each member of the group understood the importance of their role in continuing the traditions upon which the very survival of the tribe depended. The storyteller also was an entertainer, retelling familiar tales around the campfire and engaging the imaginations of all those in the circle.

As demonstrated by the stories in this book, an effective corporate story must be authentic. An authentic story reveals the true personality of the organization—in effect, its heart and soul—and it emerges from the corporate values and guiding principles that drive everyday decisions. An elegantly simple concept, storytelling as a tool for business leaders can seem simplistic; however, a well-planned, successfully implemented storytelling system can be complex, and its impact is often underestimated. To be effective, a story must be focused on a clear objective; and to achieve the objective, the story to be shared must be carefully selected, constructed, and delivered.

Authentic Stories Support and Sustain Success

What is it that makes stories so compelling? Why do you enjoy retelling some stories again and again, either to yourself or to whomever will listen? What makes a particular story not only entertaining but also unforgettable? Most of us spend little time, if any, analyzing our favorite stories; it's simply enough to appreciate them and enjoy both remembering and retelling them. Whether they're stories remembered fondly from childhood, or tales heard as recently as last week, the stories that stick with us share several characteristics. No matter the topic or structural details, a good story touches the heart by involving the reader or the audience in the main character's efforts to overcome an obstacle. The obstacle may be as simple as mastering the details of planning a family wedding, or it may be as complex as identifying the cause of a major loss of market share. Whether or not any member of the audience has had exactly the same experience, everyone has faced challenges, both simple and complex. When a story is told effectively, the audience identifies with the main character because his/her dilemma represents their obstacles, and the audience becomes engaged in the struggle to overcome them. Stories give us hope that we too can overcome the challenge we face. And either directly or indirectly, stories teach a valuable lesson about life. The best also pack a powerful wallop by conjuring up long-forgotten memories and evoking deep emotions.

To ensure that employees and associates at all levels are captivated by the vision, leaders must tell the core story consistently and often. It isn't a one-shot effort. Employees need frequent and consistent communication, especially in our era of rapid change. Contrary to the popular belief that "no news is good news," no news in a corporate setting is destructive—particularly when rumors are flying. People who know changes are coming, or who are anxious to learn whether rumors are true, want to know how the impending changes will affect their own departments and jobs. They need to be kept in the loop on a regular basis.

To engage employees in the corporate mission, leaders also must give them permission to share their own perspectives of the vision. This can be done by creating venues for employees to share their own workplace stories that illustrate the organization's values, teamwork, and successes. When they tell their own stories, they're investing themselves in the corporate values, which is beneficial to employees and the company alike. Work teams who share stories work together better, support one another more willingly, and serve the customer more effectively. As evidenced by The Container Store's experience, a company with a consistently told, authentic story is able to cut through the clutter of the highly competitive marketplace and attract customers who become enthusiastic evangelists for the organization.

Stories Not Just for Good News

During major transitions, such as mergers and/or management shake-ups, layoffs, or lagging sales, daily messages from the CEO are critical to employees' sense of security. Even when there's bad news, effective storytelling makes it easier for people to accept. When executives share the company's current situation in detail and explain the reasons for their decisions, employees are able to put themselves in the executives' shoes and understand their actions. Most people will remain supportive of the organization and will continue to be productive—and even protective of the company. And well-informed employees can be trusted.

This principle became amazingly clear when a partner and I were providing PR counsel to a municipal corporation in the midst of a major reorganization. The new structure called for a significant change in the executive offices, reallocation of responsibilities among several departments, job reassignments, and workforce reductions. The restructuring process had been underway for nearly two years, and the impending announcement of the outcome was public knowledge. The first order of business in our announcement plan was to inform employees—the people who would be most affected by the restructuring. As the key players on the corporate team, they deserved to hear the facts from the executives before anyone else.

We scheduled an employee meeting at each location the day of the announcement and a news conference for the end of the day. The executive team explained the reorganization, distributed new organization charts and newsletters explaining the changes in detail, and asked employees to keep the information to themselves until after the news conference. Even though reporters waited outside each employee meeting and pressed people for information, not one person divulged even a small detail. By sharing all the information with employees first, the executive team galvanized support for their decisions and strengthened the management-employee bond.

Conversely, when people feel shut out, they begin to believe that management can't be trusted, and morale and productivity drop. As a sales manager in one of my workshops pointed out, we aren't afraid of change per se, as we tend to believe we are. Rather, we fear not being prepared for impending change. When a leader repeatedly tells and enacts a values-based story, everyone becomes familiar with it, understands their role in keeping it alive, and develops trust in the organization's stated values.

Identifying Core Values

Faith Popcorn, originator of The Popcorn Report, was referring to the rise of values-based investing and marketing when she said, "It used to be enough just to make a fairly decent product and market it. Not anymore. You've got to have a Corporate Soul. The consumer will want to know who you are before buying what you sell." If you aren't able to readily identify your core values, start the soul-searching process by asking such questions as, What is our company's guiding principle? Is it to empower employees to do whatever it takes to deliver on our promise like FedEx? To challenge employees to take risks and be innovative like 3M? To keep everyone focused on our founder's vision like Nike?

Whatever your guiding principle(s), everyone associated with your organization should know—and be able to articulate—your organization's core values, and they also should be able to discern how they individually benefit from being a part of it. If the answer isn't readily apparent, a series of questions in the Appendix will provide a framework to guide your executive/managerial team in developing the definitive answers. For those who would like the help of a facilitator, the Appendix also includes information on how to arrange for a customized Corporate Storytelling® system to assist you in discovering your values and articulating your story or set of stories.

Visionary Companies Lead the Way

In terms of private companies competing in the marketplace, those that come up with the answers to the questions that Corporate Storytelling poses—those that are clear about what makes them unique and can clearly articulate the difference—are likely to be 15 times more successful than companies that don't articulate, and operate from, a clear vision. And they'll be six times more successful than their competitors. James C. Collins and Jerry I. Porras reported those findings in their highly regarded book, *Built to Last, Successful Habits of Visionary Companies*, written while both were teaching at Stanford University's Graduate School of Business. Conducting a six-year study of 18 "truly exceptional and long-lasting" companies with an average age of nearly 100 years, the two compared each company with one of its top competitors. They examined the companies from their very beginnings to the present day—as startups, as midsize companies, and as large corporations. Their overriding question was, "What makes truly exceptional companies different from other companies?"

They found that the two common ingredients that differentiated the leading "visionary" companies were:

- Clearly articulated core values (deeply held beliefs analogous to an individual's philosophy of life)
- A mission (a reason for being)

By defining, refining, and constantly telling its story, an organization gains clarity about its values, communicates more effectively to its stakeholders, and helps everyone in its circle to maintain focus on the vision. Repeatedly telling the story reignites the spark that fueled the organization, draws current stakeholders closer, and attracts new stakeholders who share the organization's values.

In his keynote presentation at the 2003 National Storytelling Network's conference, Syd Lieberman quoted an elderly resident of a nursing home who had shared with him some of her favorite experiences. Asked to define the most important aspect of a successful life, she asked in return, "If, at the end of your life, you don't have stories, what have you got?"

The same question applies to the life of an organization, as pointed out by Costco CEO Jim Sinegal when discussing the value of storytelling for managers. If you don't have stories that draw stakeholders into your circle and keep them there, what have you got?

Appendix A
Guide To Identifying Your Core Story

Identifying your core story is tough. It's difficult to take time out from a busy schedule to sit back, relax, let your hair down, and reflect on what's unique about your company, what your values are, and what your vision is. But it's absolutely critical to the success of your communications and the success of your business.

In today's increasingly crowded marketplace, where many of us are suffering from information overload, the ability to cut through the clutter distinguishes successful companies. An effectively targeted communications campaign (getting the right messages to the right people at the right time) is the catalyst for firing up sales and fueling growth.

A memorable story, symbol and/or phrase, such as The Container Store's man-in-the-desert myth, the 3M logo, or Nike's "Just do it," communicates who the company is and what qualities set it apart from the crowd. A clear core message will ensure that the investment in your communications campaigns will pay off with the results you want.

To be effective, your communication campaign needs to reach the right audience(s)...with the right message(s)...through the most effective media...making the best use of resources...to produce the desired results.

Here are some questions to help you get started with defining or refining your core story:

- Who are we now?

- What are the core values on which we base everyday decisions?

- Who were we five years ago?

- Who do we want to be five years from now?

- Who are our key audiences (employees, stockholders, etc.)?

- What do our audiences want and need to know about us?

- How do they like to hear from us?

If you're uncertain about the answer to any of these questions, there's one more you need to address: How are you going to clarify your company's core message so everyone—employees, customers, affiliates, suppliers, stockholders—will have the same view of your organization?

For help clarifying your core story, schedule a Corporate Storytelling keynote, retreat or workshop led by Evelyn Clark, The Corporate Storyteller.

Call toll-free: 1-866-818-8079
E-mail: evelyn@corpstory.com
Web site: www.corpstory.com

Appendix B
Checklist for Evaluating Your Own Storytelling

The following checklist will help you measure how well you are supporting management goals and objectives through your current storytelling efforts. Because each item on this list is a critical component of a well-designed communication plan, spaces are provided for you to schedule target dates for adding elements that are missing or strengthening those that need improvement.

Employee Communications	Yes	No	Goal Date
Corporate mission is clearly understood and regularly reinforced.			
Employees are the first to be informed of new policies, appointments, and news.			
Supervisors and managers meet with employees on a regular schedule and are accessible for unscheduled interaction.			
Leaders encourage feedback and listen carefully, taking appropriate action accordingly.			
Employees at all levels are empowered to make decisions within the widest parameters possible.			
Rewards are based on what employees want.			

Business Communications	Yes	No	Goal Date
Affiliates and business associates are familiar with the organization's mission.			
Involvement with trade and industry groups is consistent with our stated mission.			
Participation in professional and trade groups is supported for employees at all levels.			
Memberships are undertaken with a commitment to regularly contribute time and effort.			
A detailed media crisis plan is ready in case the organization experiences a business crisis or becomes the focus of negative publicity.			
Customer Communications			
Key audiences are clearly identified, with core messages targeted specifically to each one.			
Appropriate media are used for reaching each audience.			
Advertising, sales, and marketing materials convey a consistent message and readily identifiable image.			
Web site is updated regularly, easy to navigate, and fully operational 24/7.			
Audiences are encouraged to give honest feedback on how the company can best serve them.			
Management listens carefully to feedback and takes appropriate action accordingly.			

Community Relations	Yes	No	Goal Date
Our organization is a "good neighbor" i.e., company and employees contribute time and financial support to community groups.			
A detailed emergency plan is ready in case of disasters, such as earthquake, fire, personal injury, etc.			
Media relations is ongoing, with trained spokespersons prepared for and engaging in regular contact with trade and news media.			
Executives and other management officials are accessible and openly participate with neighbors and the community at large on issues of mutual interest.			

Appendix C
Corporate Story Template

Everyone can become a more effective communicator and hone leadership skills by learning to tell a good story. The following template will get you started, and once you begin, you'll discover how much fun storytelling is, especially if you work with a group of your peers. You'll spark one another's ideas and everyone will benefit from the brainstorm.

Develop your own personal story collection and update it regularly, mixing a few fresh tales with old favorites that you know always work. That way, you'll always be prepared with an appropriate story when you're called upon to address a group.

Story Title

The title is like a news headline; it needs to be a "grabber" that hooks people's interest. Play up a detail of the story, add an unexpected twist, or exaggerate the facts. Let yourself have some fun with a straightforward occurrence, such as David Armstrong's "The Day I Paid $248,000 to Play a Round of Golf" or call out the dramatic element of an experience, such as, "Dad, I Saved A Life Today."

Here are some thought-starters:
"The Day I Learned ______________________________."
"My Heart Nearly Stopped When__________________."
"Who Would Believe ______________________________?"

The Challenge

Every good story is built on an unusual situation, removing the obstacle to a goal, or overcoming a seemingly insurmountable challenge. It can be as momentous as starting a company or as simple as finding your keys. People who always have stories about their day don't have unusually eventful lives. They take note of ordinary challenges in daily life and recount them in entertaining ways.

In the space below, jot down the amusing or frustrating experiences that happen during an ordinary day. Look at each experience from the perspective of each person involved and probe the situation for irony, conflict, humor, and/or insight.

After you develop stories based on these experiences, list the number of topics each story can be related to and the number of lessons that can be drawn from it.

The Problem-Solving Approach

Explain how you and/or your work team or department *found a solution*. When and where appropriate, include bits of humor. A funny story is highly memorable, and a witty comment inserted periodically in a serious story provides necessary comic relief. One seminar leader started a program for professional speakers by telling about the time he spilled an entire glass of water on his lap just before he was introduced as the keynote speaker at an executive dinner.

How did you overcome a potentially humiliating or embarrassing situation?

What did you say when your laptop crashed in the middle of your presentation on the wonders of technology?

When someone said or did something that rendered you speechless, what did you do?

The Solution

Briefly and clearly describe how you and/or your work team or department *met the challenge*.

The Results/Payoff

Explain the impact of your actions on customer service, fulfilling the company's mission, and/or the bottom line (increased efficiency, higher revenue, customer retention, etc.) Tie the point to the core value you want to emphasize.

Construct the Story

Now put it all together by writing a rough draft:

Title: ____

When we realized that (or were asked to)____(challenge)______,

my work group/department brainstormed solutions by

__(your approach)__________. We decided to ____(solution)___.

This is a great example of what we mean when we say

___(core value)_________________.

Appendix D
Studies On Essential Workplace Learning

In 1998 The Center for Workforce Development published The Teaching Firm Study[1] that detailed a six year research project which studied the question, "Where does essential learning happen in the workplace?" This was an ambitious and comprehensive study that partnered major corporations and their counterpart state agencies relating to corporate employment. Corporations such as Boeing, Data Instruments, Motorola and Siemens were participants in the study along with their state governmental agencies in Washington, Connecticut, North Carolina, and Massachusetts. The major research finding of the study was that up to 70% of the new skills, information and competence in the workplace is acquired through informal learning. Informal learning is defined as a learning process that is neither determined nor defined by the organization.

That is, the essential job competency learning regarding professional/technical, intrapersonal, interpersonal, and organizational/cultural learnings and skills were learned informally. The activities in which this informal learning occurred were identified as team settings, mentoring, peer communication, and between-shift communication. All of these activities are platforms for transmission of essential job knowledge and skills through storytelling. Other researchers

---

[1]*The Teaching Firm Where Productive Work and Learning Converge*, The Center for Workforce Development, Newton, MA, 1998.

refer to storytelling as "jointly told tales" and "learning histories". What we find in this research is that storytelling is the bedrock of informal learning.

In another study Seely Brown[2] describes the research of an anthropologist studying a service organization who found that the essential job skill knowledge was transmitted informally around the coffee pot and lunch through storytelling rather than in the training classroom. He said, "In a sense these stories are the real 'expert systems' used by the tech-reps on the job. They are a storehouse of past problems and diagnoses, a template for constructing a theory about the current problem, and the basis for making an educated stab at a solution. By creating such stories and constantly refining them through conversation with each other, tech-reps are creating a powerful 'organizational memory' that is a valuable resource for the company."

Finally, Kleiner and Roth[3] cite four reasons why storytelling is effective in organizations:

1. Stories build trust. People who believe their opinions were ignored in the past come to feel these opinions validated when they experience them articulated in a story.
2. Stories are effective at raising issues that people want to talk about but have not had the courage to discuss openly.
3. Stories have proves successful at transferring knowledge from one part of the organization to another.

---

[2]Seely Brown, John, "Research That Reinvents the Corporation," *Harvard Business Review*, January-February 1991.

[3]Kleiner, Art and Roth, George, "How to Make Experience Your Company's Best Teacher," *Harvard Business Review*, September-October 1997.

4. Stories help build a body of generalizable knowledge about corporate management and leadership, about what works and what doesn't.

Recommended Reading

Armstrong, David, *Managing by Storying Around*, Armstrong International, 1992.

Bennett, Julie, "Spin Straw Into Gold With Good Storytelling," *Startup Journal*, The Wall Street Journal Center for Entrepreneurs, WSJ.com, July 2003.

Bennett, Julie, "Promoting Diversity Through Storytelling," *Career Journal,* The Wall Street Journal, WSJ.com, July 2003.

Campbell, Joseph, *The Power of Myth*, Doubleday, 1998.

Collins, James C. and Jerry I. Porras, *Built to Last: Successful Habits of Visionary Companies*, HarperBusiness, 1994.

Collins, Jim, *Good to Great: Why Some Companies Make the Leap…and Others Don't,* HarperColllins, 2001.

Cory, Diane and Paula Underwood, "Stories for Learning: Exploring Your Circumstance," *Learning Organizations: Developing Cultures for Tomorrow's Workplace*, Productivity Press, Inc., September 1995.

Denning, Steve, *The Springboard: How Storytelling Ignites Action in Knowledge-Era Organizations*, Butterworth-Heinemann, October 2000.

De Pree, Max, *Leadership Is An Art*, Currency, August 1989.

"Dream Society," *Fast Company,* October 1999.

"Fast Take," *Fast Company,* April 2000.

Fulford, Robert, *The Triumph of Narrative: Storytelling in the Age of Mass Culture,* Broadway Books, February 2001.

Gabriel, Yiannis, *Storytelling in Organizations: Facts, Fictions, and Fantasies*, Oxford University Press, July 2000.

Gunther, Marc, "God and Business," *Fortune,* cover story, July 9, 2001, p.58.

Henry, Linda G. and James D. Henry, *The Soul of the Physician: Doctors Speaking about Passion, Resilience, and Hope,* American Medical Association, January 2002.

Lipman, Doug, *Basics for All Who Tell Stories in Work or Play*, August House, June 1999.

Maister, David H., *Practice What You Preach*, The Free Press, 2001.

Neuhauser, Peg C., *Corporate Legends and Lore*, McGraw-Hill Trade, May 1993.

Ready, Douglas A., "How Storytelling Builds Next-Generation Leaders," *MIT Sloan Management Review*, Summer 2002, p. 63.

"Religion in the Workplace: The growing presence of spirituality in Corporate America," *Business Week,* November 2, 1999.

Shaw, Gordon, Robert Brown, and Philip Bromiley, "Strategic Stories: How 3M Is Rewriting Business Planning," *Harvard Business Review*, May 1998.

Simmons, Annette, *The Story Factor: Inspiration, Influence, and Persuasion through the Art of Storytelling*, Perseus Books, 2000.

Spirit in Business, www.spiritinbusiness.net/quotes.

Stevenson, Doug, *Never Be Boring Again: Make Your Business Presentations Capture Attention, Inspire Action, and Produce Results*, Cornelia Press, 2004.

Stone, Richard, *The Healing Art of Storytelling: A Sacred Journey of Personal Discovery*, Hyperion, October 1996.

"Storytelling That Moves People: A Conversation with Screenwriting Coach Robert McKee," *Harvard Business Review*, June 2003, p. 51.

Wacker, Mary and Lori Silverman, *Stories Trainers Tell: 55 Ready-to-Use Stories to Make Training Stick*, Jossey-Bass/Pfeiffer, 2003.

Weil, Elizabeth, "Every Leader Tells A Story," *Fast Company*, June 1998, p. 38.

Index

About the Author

Evelyn Clark, The Corporate Storyteller, works with leaders and work teams who want to develop and tell powerful stories that inspire and sustain success. She has generated results for global and industry leaders such as Microsoft, World Vision, Costco, CH2M Hill, and VeriSign.

Evelyn delivers keynote addresses, conducts customized workshops, and facilitates retreats focused on developing values-based stories and communication platforms that increase sales, maximize teamwork, and enhance organizational effectiveness. She contributed the corporate stories for the book, *TechnoBrands,* and has published numerous articles on communication management and public relations.

Selected by her peers to present a workshop at the 2004 National Storytelling Network Conference, Evelyn is also a member of the National Speakers Association. A Communications graduate of the University of Washington, she began her career as a broadcast news editor for the Associated Press and has earned accreditation from the Public Relations Society of America.